11/2013 3 —1 6/2007

Kids Helping Kids
Break the Silence of Sexual Abuse

By
Linda Lee Foltz

Lighthouse Point Press
Pittsburgh, Pennsylvania

Kids Helping Kids
Break the Silence of Sexual Abuse
By Linda Lee Foltz

Published by:

LIGHTHOUSE
POINT PRESS

Lighthouse Point Press
100 First Avenue, Suite 525
Pittsburgh, PA 15222

This publication is designed to provide accurate and authoritative information in regard to the subject matter covered. Its purpose is to educate and inform, and is not meant to replace conventional therapy, but rather to support prevention, intervention and therapy.

Names of individuals and identifying information in the book have been changed at their request.

The author and Lighthouse Point Press shall have neither liability nor responsibility to any person or entity with respect to any loss or damage caused, or alleged to be caused, directly or indirectly by the information contained in this book.

Copyright © 2003 by Linda Lee Foltz
Printed in the United States of America
Library of Congress Control Number: 2003100215

Publisher's Cataloging in Publication Data
Foltz, Linda Lee
Kids Helping Kids: Break the Silence of Sexual Abuse
        p.   cm.

1.   Sexual Abuse   j 362.76
2.   Recovery
3.   Self-help
ISBN 0-9637966-9-0: $14.95 Softcover
ISBN 0-9637966-8-2: $21.95 Hardcover
This book is printed on acid-free stock
First Printing, March 2003

Acknowledgements

This book is dedicated to Erica Harkema who selflessly devoted her life to protecting children. Although few will ever know all the sacrifices she made, lives she touched or children she saved, her accomplishments will forever be noted by the three white rosebuds and youthful handwritten card that lay at the foot of her coffin. It read: *Thank you for saving my life.*

Without Erica, many children would have died.

Without Erica, this book of hope and healing would never have been written.

Table of Contents

Introduction for Parents

Parents are essential for children to heal from child abuse. This book would not be complete without addressing their perspective. The discovery of serious injury of a child is very painful and traumatic for parents. After fifteen years of psychotherapy with abused children and families, I remain speechless about its horrors. However, I have also learned to marvel at the healing that routinely occurs. Children are both fragile and resilient. Their pain and hurt is raw and exposed. Yet, their capacity to forgive and overcome is refreshing and unending. When asked how I withstand the pain of so many stories of abuse, I reply with accounts of healing and revelation. So much of life's beauty emerges when humans are challenged by the worst possible horrors. The world does not end with child abuse. Through the pain and suffering, a different life comes forth than what was dreamed of and visualized at the child's birth. In many ways, it is a better life than ever before imagined.

Many parents mistakenly direct the lives of abused children. Captured by their fear and pain, these parents smother their children and limit their growth. They view children as broken and emptied. The exposed ravages of their child's agony overwhelm their senses. They see them and imagine themselves wrenched with unbounded pain. Children are treated as if they are forever tainted and scared. It is their second loss of innocence. While smothering immediately after disclosure is healthy and normal, a sustained over-focus on children jeopardizes their long-term health.

Children recover from pain and abuse. They have a natural drive to regulate and guide their lives by dreams, plans and goals. Another natural force pushes them to connect with others and have meaningful relationships. These forces are constant currents that flow through all of our lives. No child, parent or psychotherapist invents healing. When the relationships in life support it, children spontaneously search for meaning and intimacy, and find a healthy perspective on their abuse. They find ways of using the pain to forge humanitarian values and a tremendous empathy for others. Instead of pain ending, healing fuels it into a determination to make life dense with significance and purpose. In our often cold, violent and distant culture, abused and healed children are our salvation. They become the people I most admire and wish to emulate.

When asked by parents how to help their children heal, I direct attention to their own lives. Healthy parents create healing emotional environments and relationships for children. These parents do not do anything specific to their children. Instead, they build an emotional reservoir of skills, support and knowledge for children to tap when needed. They remain available and do not intrude into the healing process. They let their children hurt and find words for awful experiences. Children have the emotional space to weave their own web of new ideas and views of themselves and others that allow them to move past abuse. Healthy parents have friends and family members who support their pain and healing. These parents take full ownership of their role in assuring children are safe. Managing themselves is a very important priority for parents assisting their child's healing process.

The challenges and obstacles for parents are many. They

are manageable, and thousands of parents have walked the path before you. In many communities, there are resources and services to provide supports. Below is a summary of challenges and issues.

Seek Knowledge and Information About Trauma and Abuse – Over the past two decades, an abundance of literature has emerged as resources for parents and children. I routinely suggest parents explore their local bookstore and library for literary resources that fit their level of interest, knowledge and psychological sophistication. Knowledge and information increases our ability to not personalize the experiences and behavior of our children. We better prepare for the future challenges and stages of healing and growth. Literature on trauma, stress, child abuses, psychotherapy and sexual assault is useful. General literature is available at national chain booksellers. Information that is more technical is available at university libraries and bookstores. Rape crisis centers, victims of crime support centers and child abuse treatment programs are widely available resources for literature and support.

Avoid Emotional Isolation and Develop Supports – Parents and families are emotionally isolated when there are few relationships available to manage the important survival and emotional issues, and conflicts routinely occurring in our lives. We can know hundreds of people and have little emotional support. When emotionally isolated, it is difficult for parents to adequately manage their anger, pain and fear. In simple terms, parents must remain calmer than their children in order to be an effective resource and support to them.

Extending beyond the secrecy and boundaries of family is important to gaining emotional support and avoiding isolation. There are seemingly hundreds of reasons to not reach out to extended family, friends and professionals. However, isolation and secrecy is a common aspect of child abuse. Parents must demonstrate for their children how networks of friends and family supports are essential to navigating the challenges of stress, conflict and healing. The road to healing is long and difficult. It will drain even the strongest person who dares to travel alone.

Develop and Build Conflict Management Skills – Child abuse and its disclosure is traumatic for all members of the family. No one proceeds in life as they did before. Spouses, grandparents, children and other relatives have to re-negotiate relationship responsibilities and roles. When a family member perpetrates the abuse, these changes and challenges are even greater. With families that avoid conflict, or with families that become highly conflictual and aggressive, changes in family relationships trigger escalating and intense stresses and additional traumas. What often emerges is divorce, marital distance, relationship cutoff between generations, and emotional withdrawal.

One member of a family, dedicated to decreasing and more responsibly managing his or her immature responses to others, can make a significant difference in how conflict and shifting relationships are managed. This behavior avoids the escalation of distance, avoidance and aggression that threaten safety and trust. Relationships remain engaged longer, and this increases the opportunity for conflict resolution, and decreases the risk of tensions becoming chronic. Unresolved conflicts and tensions erode the quality of family and social relationships necessary for healing and recovery from abuse. Seek professional services when conflict results in sustained relationship distance, conflict and cutoff between generations.

Decrease Blaming and Denying of Family Problems – The extent to which family members regulate and manage their emotional responses to one another is a measure of better individual and family functioning. Denial and blaming are opposite characteristics of self-regulation. Parents who manage their strong and intense emotional responses to the abuse and disclosure become a resource to children. Denial and blaming perpetuate intense responses either by ignoring and minimizing them or by holding others responsible. Many children find the violence of the abuse is less traumatic than the years of stress, conflict and turmoil triggered by disclosure and its aftermath. Both denial and blame make families continually unsafe places. Children continue to use the psychological defenses and symptoms they developed to manage their abuse. Healing is aborted and stymied. This fuels more family tensions and conflicts. Distortions of responsibility are common in families when child abuse and violence occur.

Distinguishing all of the layers of responsibility in family relationships is complex and challenging. Abusers are responsible for their violent acts, no matter what good reasons exist for their behavior. Children and other family members are not responsible for triggering abuse and violence even if we all were to find the child's behavior difficult and frustrating. Each child and family member is responsible for finding his or her way of healing from the violence. Each of us is responsible for respecting the unique way others heal. Parents and other adults are responsible for assuring the safety of children, even if they are older teens. Parents are the leaders of families and they are to guide and demonstrate healthy ways of managing stresses and nurturing others.

Identify Multi-Generational Patterns of Abuse and Violence – Parents with histories of child abuse are greatly challenged to well manage the abuse of their children. Parents who are healed are great assets to children. Their experience and knowledge will be a life raft when their children are rocked by waves of anger, pain and grief. Parents who denied and minimized their own abuse will greatly struggle watching their children hurt and suffer. Distinguishing between their child's emotions and their own becomes very difficult and impossible at times. Quietly, children learn that their pain triggers their parent's pain, and the quality of the healing emotional environment is compromised. Children's lives become organized around minimizing their parent's pains.

Often I have witnessed sexual and physical abuse stop, and domestic violence and verbal abuse escalate. Any form of violence compromises safety and healing. I define violence as aggression that controls the functioning of others. It may be verbal, physical, emotional, sexual or the omission of care for a dependent person. Long-term patterns of violent behavior in families require professional services and supports in order to promote healing and health.

Minimize the Number and Severity of Other Stressors – Disclosure frequently occurs in the midst of other stresses and traumatic events. Many parents are overwhelmed by the changes that occur before and after disclosure. Legal, financial, medical and psychological problems make an already overwhelming situation a nightmare. Many families with problems of child abuse have problems with alcohol, drug abuse and addiction.

The first task for parents is to create safety. Children develop symptoms and problems as a way of protecting and coping. They continue to need these symptoms until they are safe. Safety is eliminating the risk of child abuse (and other forms of violence) from re-occurring. Safety comes before treatment and healing. The second task is to assure that family, social and professional supports are in place. In the initial stages of healing, children and family members typically deny and suppress feelings and experiences of injury and pain. All members of the nuclear family need support, even if they are children who do not directly know of the abuse. Changes in family relationships after disclosure impact all family members. The third task is to develop a long-term plan of action that prioritizes and schedules decisions and challenges. Avoid stressful decisions that result in little consequence if delayed. Prioritize decisions that create stress but increase family safety and stability over long periods. Create a plan for personal learning, support and growth. Negotiate a separate one with your family.

Healing from the wounds of child abuse takes years. Healing does not mean the pain goes away. It becomes manageable and does not interfere with our ability to achieve a meaningful life and do important things. In the final stages of healing, the pain of abuse is so incorporated into our lives that we cannot imagine that we would have the strength of determination, will and perseverance we possess without it. Yet, at each important developmental stage and important life event, the pain re-emerges. It remains in our peripheral vision throughout our lives, neither a blinding glare nor the quiet blindness of denial. It becomes more fuel and determination for doing our best in life.

Children need parental leadership and health to heal. They need safe and nurturing relationships that foster their freedom to explore and discover their unique ways of making sense of their trauma. In providing these things, they will travel their own path of healing. Life will never be the same. However, it has the very real potential of being even better.

Walter Howard Smith, Jr., Ph.D.
Psychologist

Introduction for Kids

Your first thought when you saw the title of this book may have been, "I don't want to read that book." The thought of you or one of your friends being hurt in a way that involves sex is painful and embarrassing. I would like to ask you to read this book and give it a chance to speak to you. This book is written in the voices of other children like you, children who just want to be loved and have others love them.

The things said in this book are stories you can learn from. I really think that kids help other kids very well if they are able to talk to each other. The first place you may go with a problem will be to your friends and your friends will try to help you. Child abuse is usually a *secret*. A *secret* is an important thing to you, and I know that. What is so cool about this book is that other kids are able to tell you their *secrets* so that you can learn from them and know what to do if you or someone you know is in trouble. Lots of children have told me their *secrets*, and I am honored and grateful to them for doing so. I feel that I can help them once I know the dangers they face.

Can you think for a minute of what you feel like when you tell a scary *secret*? You know how your tummy feels queasy and your head hurts and you just want to be left alone? *Secrets* and untruths are what keep alive the abuse that happens to kids. You can be a part of fighting back at child abuse when you learn about it and try to understand it.

Knowledge is power and power can keep you SAFE.

Lots of times kids feel as if they have no control over their lives, and they are correct when they think that. Adults do have more power than kids, and are able to convince kids to do things they do not want to do. When adults are trying to teach children how to live in the world, they often have to teach children how to do things they might not want to do. When a child starts questioning everything a parent says, that means they are trying out their wings so they can fly on their own. Do you sometimes want to fly on your own? This book, and what it tells you, can help you fly more safely. There are many safe adults in your life. Maybe you could pick one of the safe adults in your life and ask them to read this book with you. If the stories in this book bother you, then you should talk about it. The stories in this book can also help parents understand what happens to kids and what it feels like.

When adults abuse children, they are using power over them that is hurtful. Children are able to take that power back, and heal, when the *secret* is out of its hiding place. Lots of kids tell me that they feel so much better after they tell their *secret*, but they are scared that other people might think what happened to them was their fault. The stories in this book will help you understand that abuse is not the fault of the child.

You kids are so strong, and I am so very proud to know all of you and to be a part of so many of your lives. Kids have taught me how to hope and how to believe in healing. No matter what happens to you, you can get better and become a better person in the end.

S – *Secrets* make you scared. Remember that if a *secret* makes your inside feel funny, it may not be a good *secret* to keep.

E – Excellence is in all people. You are an excellent person. Believe in yourself.

C – Coping with hard times is something that all children have to do. Learning about yourself will help you cope well with life and all of the hard parts of growing up.

R – Responsibility is a hard thing in life. Both children and grown-ups are responsible for their own actions.

E – Exposing truths is hard, and this information is hard to read, but it will help you.

T – Terrific kids, like you, are everywhere around the world, trying to grow up and have a happy life.

Let's stop the *secrets*
Take time to think about "Kids Helping Kids"
Let's break the silence together
Be brave and learn
Kids are the bravest people I know.

Sincerely,
Erica Harkema, MSW, LSW
Clinical Forensic Manager

Chapter 1

Stranger Dangers and People You Know

Katie's Story

My name is Katie. I grew up in a typical, middle-class family. We lived in a very safe neighborhood, which was so kid friendly. There was a neighborhood swimming pool, and my older brother and I were on the swim team. All the neighbors would gather and just hang out at the pool. We had block parties, birthday parties, and my brother and I would go into these woods and build tepees and stuff, and pretend we were Indians.

If I fell down, I wanted my dad to come to save his little "Pup." That's what he called me. But with any other problems, I wanted my mom. She and I were best friends. I could talk to her about everything, from the color of my underwear to anything. All my friends were envious of our relationship. During this time in my life, I remember myself just being so happy, almost floating. My family was everything I wanted them to be – storybook perfect. But that didn't last forever. I was eight when everything changed.

I adored my brother. He was three years older, and I always wanted to hang out with him. Usually he didn't want me around, but one day, his friends weren't home and he said he wanted to spend time with me. I was so happy. I don't know how I did it, but I got him to play house with me.

After playing house, we started playing doctor. I was the doctor. I checked his heart and his throat, and the next thing I knew he pulled down his pants. He wanted me to check him "there." I said, "ew…no." I told him I didn't want to. He said something like, "Man, Katie, I thought you were my favorite sister. I was really starting to think you were cool. I was even thinking about playing Monopoly with you after we played doctor, but I guess not."

Monopoly was my favorite board game. Besides, all I really wanted was my brother's attention. I started to think he might never play with me again. I started to feel guilty. So when he lay on the bed, motioning for me to do it, I started to touch him, massaging like he wanted. I just felt so dirty and disgusted, and I really didn't want to do it. I was terrible at it, and right away my brother got really mad at me.

He yelled, then laughed at me. He made me feel like I was an idiot for not knowing how to please him. I felt like nothing, like a fool, and I just couldn't do it anymore. Crying, I ran into the bathroom and locked the door. I couldn't even look at myself in the mirror. I started to wash my hands. I probably washed them ten, twenty times – I just wanted to wash it away, but I couldn't. I still felt dirty.

After five sexual encounters with my brother, the game

became sexual toward me. He forced me to "please" him sexually. He touched my body, instead of having me touch his. I didn't let myself think about the things going on between us. I remember focusing on the night-light and the way the trees waved to me from outside my bedroom window. I memorized the details of the beautiful, pastel flowers on the base of the lamp next to my bed, and I remember the way my brother's eyes looked as he was doing it. Sometimes I'd feel pain, but most of the time I just removed myself, and wouldn't allow myself to know what was actually happening.

One day, during this time when my brother was abusing me, our neighbors accused him of doing it to their little boy, too. I remember sitting on the stairs that led up to the family room listening to a conversation between my parents and neighbors. The little boy said my brother touched him in private places. My dad got so fuming angry. He stormed out of the house, picked my brother up from school and sat him down at the kitchen table. My dad yelled at my brother about what the neighbors had accused him of. My mom talked and cried.

I remember thinking YES. Go get him, Dad. Good job, Mom. Way to stand up for me, well, sort of. I was so happy they gave it to him big time. I went to bed on cloud nine. I really thought my parents had taken care of things. I thought things were going to change for me. But my brother was never punished, the neighbor never pressed charges, and in just a few days, things went right back to the way they were – he kept abusing me.

After that I became very submissive. I turned all of my

emotions inside. I felt like it was entirely my fault. I knew what my brother and I were doing was wrong, but I wanted him to love me. I needed to believe he wanted to be the best big brother in the world.

I thought the world of my parents, too. I just wanted them to love me like they loved my brother. I couldn't understand why they would love and protect him so much and leave me out in the cold. I started resenting them a lot. They should have protected me. They should have had this vibe that told them he was sexually abusing me.

I started eating. I thought if I got big and fat and ugly, then maybe my brother would leave me alone. Maybe the food just made me feel better, I don't know. It tasted good, it gave me pleasure. I also hurt myself. I cut myself. I know it sounds crazy, but when the pain inside me was bigger than me, I'd do something to cause myself pain. Then I could think about the pain I caused, instead of the pain he caused. It probably sounds crazy, but it was a distraction, and it gave me control.

The last event I remember between my brother and me was so emotionally degrading, I just couldn't handle it any more. Afterwards, I literally shut down. I lost myself. My brother came home from school one day. He was studying the Holocaust. My parents decided to go out that evening. While babysitting me, my brother put me in my own concentration camp. It was like he thought he was Hitler, a young Hitler. He was so detached from everything. He was so cold. He forced me to get undressed and made me run repeatedly around the house, down one set of stairs and then up the other set. It was just like what I saw in a movie, like he was trying to see if I was good enough to be put in the concentration camp as a worker, or if I wasn't worth keeping and would be sent to the gas chamber to die.

When I was running past him, he yelled at me and told me how dumb I looked – how pathetic. When I was totally out of breath from running three flights of stairs over and over again, he laughed at me. Then he took advantage of me sexually, but it was the emotional stuff that really got to me.

Shortly after that, we moved and my brother turned to drugs. He stopped abusing me but it was too late. I became depressed and suicidal. I felt like I was nothing, like I deserved nothing. I could never please my brother, and I felt like a failure. In my mind I was sure I just couldn't please anybody, and I believed that nobody loved me. I even believed that if someone wanted to love me, they couldn't. I was unlovable, dirty, ashamed and guilty. I thought I was ugly. I hated myself.

The whole time the abuse was happening, I didn't tell anyone. At first I was quiet, because I knew my brother had a knife and he threatened to use it if I told. But, after the thing with the neighbors, I stayed quiet because I didn't think my parents would believe me. I was afraid if they had to choose between us, they'd believe my brother. He always seemed to get his way, and I couldn't take the risk of losing my entire family. I loved them all, including my brother, and I desperately needed them to love me.

It took me nine years to get the courage to tell someone. It was last year. I was a freshman in college and working a part-time job when the memories and the pain became too much for me to ignore anymore. That's when I took some time off from school and faced it all.

I got into counseling and, even though it was the hardest thing I ever did, my counselor helped me tell my mother. My mom cried and cried. She told me how sorry she was, and how she didn't know it was happening to me. She said if she had known, she would have done things differently. She rubbed my leg and hugged me. Then she told me she loved me. She said we'd get through this together, and she's been there for me every step of the way.

At first, counseling was really hard, but now I have found a counselor who can truly empathize with me. I think the most difficult part about counseling was reliving the pain. The good part is that, this time, I didn't have to do it alone. Now I have a great counselor and the support of my mother, and both validate my feelings. The counselor has also encouraged me to speak up and tell the world about the injustices I have lived through, and how it has made me a better person.

Counseling has also helped me gain a sense of myself. I no longer feel as much pressure to be the person everyone wants me to be. I'm trying to find myself and be myself. I'm learning my likes and dislikes, passions, inspirations, goals and dreams. I never used to own my feelings or feel entitled to have them. I never used to feel worthy of being loved, either. Now I do. It's very empowering.

I still have trouble trusting people, and I still blame myself when something goes wrong, but I'm working on that. Otherwise, for the most part, I think I'm stronger because of what I've survived. I know I can survive anything life hands me. Surviving this has also given me the drive and true ambition to help others. When I graduate from college, I'm hoping to get my Master's Degree in Social Work. In addition to helping people who have been through sibling abuse, I'd like to focus on building community awareness of it.

If I had to say what helped me get through all this, I'd say it was writing. I spent a lot of time sitting alone in my room, writing in my journal. When I was writing, I was in control and I felt safe knowing I could write down my feelings, lock them up and put them away. My journal was a place where I could release the emotions that were all pent up inside me. Because I did so much writing growing up, I think I'm fairly good at it now, and I hope to use those skills when I go to work helping others and bringing awareness to the community.

If I were going to give adults advice, I'd say, "Teach children at a very early age about sexual abuse, so kids feel as though it's an acceptable topic to discuss. Adults also need to understand that children cannot stay safe from sexual abuse if they are manipulated or forced. But if adults create a safe place for kids, kids can speak up when it happens and get safe more quickly. I'd also tell adults if one sibling abuses another, both kids need help. Believe the child who tells you what's happening, but don't treat the abusing child like a criminal. That child is screaming for help, too."

If I could give advice to kids, I'd tell them, "Tell someone, even if you think you won't be believed. Chances are someone will believe you, and if they don't, at least you stood up for yourself." I'd also tell kids, "You can't control others and the power they have over you, but you can control your attitude and how you react toward the situation. You can choose to survive."

✺✺✺

From the time you were little, you were probably taught "stranger dangers." You may have been told, "Don't talk to strangers" or "Never get into a car with someone you don't know. It isn't safe." The trusting adults who told you that were right.

Although staying away from strangers is a very good way to stay safe when it comes to sexual abuse, strangers aren't the only ones who can abuse you. In fact, the person most likely to sexually abuse you is usually NOT a stranger at all. Most of the time it's someone you know, someone you're around a lot. Often it's someone who is in charge of you.

Most of the people you know – neighbors, babysitters, coaches, friends, teachers, parents, stepparents, older brothers and sisters, and other family members – protect you and take good care of you. They would never want to touch or look at your private parts, or have you touch or look at theirs. They would never force you to do anything sexual or hurt you in a sexual way. It's okay to trust these people because they understand how to have healthy relationships with children and teens.

But a few people cannot be trusted. These people don't know how to have healthy relationships with children and teens. *They will want you to look at or touch their private parts, or want to look at or touch yours. They might try to force you to do something sexual, or they might hurt you in a sexual way. They are called abusers. Abusers look and act just like all the people who live around them. The only difference is that they develop slow, trusting relationships with children that allow them to have time alone with kids and eventually trick or force kids into sexual activity.*

Remember: Although staying away from strangers is a good way to stay safe, when it comes to sexual abuse, the person most likely to abuse you is usually someone you know and trust. Often it's someone who is in charge of you.

Chapter 2

Anyone Can Be an Abuser

Lee's Story

Growing up, I lived with my dad, mom and younger sister. We always had money and lots of nice things, whatever we needed – whatever we wanted. When I turned 16, my dad even bought me a brand new sports car. But, just because we had money didn't mean life was easy. It wasn't. Both my parents drank too much. My dad was rarely home and when he was, he was mean, even verbally abusive. My little sister and I didn't get along, either. She blamed me for everything.

When I was seven years old, I was cutting between two garages on my way to meet my best friend. We were going to play baseball in the field about a block away. These three teenage girls, who lived in the neighborhood, were at the end of the garage in the alley, like they were waiting for someone. They grabbed me and pulled me over. One pushed my shoulders against the concrete wall, one held my ankles, and the other dropped my pants. They touched me and licked me in private places and put my private part in their mouth. I was terrified.

It went on for a long time. They'd wait for me in the alley and if I'd take another route, like through the park or something, they'd be there, too, waiting for me. They'd take turns on me. Once they even tried to have sex with me.

Even though I was a boy and they were girls, they were too strong for me. I was only seven. They were 15 or 16, and a lot bigger. I didn't have much of a chance trying to resist them.

I told my best friend Joey about it right away. He said I had to tell an adult. I wanted to tell someone, but I felt like I didn't have anyone to tell. I mean I wanted to tell my mother mostly, but she was drinking a lot then and not really there for me. I couldn't tell my father, because, well, he wasn't home much and when he was, he would verbally abuse me. I already had a hard time trusting people, because my mother would lie about her drinking and my dad lied about where he was and why he said mean things to me. So I didn't feel like I could tell anyone what was happening, and the girls kept stalking me and doing it to me.

My parents noticed that I was really angry, but since the kids at school always picked on me, they thought that's what was wrong. I don't think my anger had anything to do with the kids at school. I think it was all because of what those girls were doing to me. I think it was because I felt like I couldn't do anything to stop them.

Besides being angry, I also became terrified of the dark. I couldn't go to bed unless the light was on. I started wetting the bed, too. I started having these awful night terrors where

I'd wake up in the middle of the night thinking the girls were there in my room and stuff. I'd scream, and my mom would come into my room to see if I was all right.

I think that might be why my mother wanted me to sleep with her; well, that and the fact that my dad was never home. Anyway, my mom never did anything sexual to me, but after I started sleeping with her, there was a lot of cuddling and hugging. She'd put my head on her chest and tell me, "You're my boy" and, "Don't ever leave me" and, "You're the man your father isn't," and that was really confusing for me.

My mom and dad weren't very close, and my dad said that was all my fault. I believed him. I felt like sleeping with my mom was, I don't know, taking her away from him. I felt really guilty about it.

One of the things I did that helped me get through everything was drawing. When I was about six, my family took me to this really nice ski resort for a vacation. I fell in love with the place the first time I was there. As soon as I got home, I started sketching it.

I had a really supportive uncle. He was a good guy, kind of a jack-of-all-trades, someone who could do anything. I looked up to him, and he always encouraged me. He stuck up for me with my father, too. He and my dad would get into arguments about me.

Anyway, my dad thought my drawing was stupid and useless, but my uncle kept telling me to go with it. Knowing he really believed in me made a big difference. I'd stay in my room for hours, even days at a time, drawing. I felt safe in my room, and I always felt better after I was done drawing, like it helped me to get out my feelings and even get rid of some of my anger.

Drawing also made me feel better about myself, because I really struggled at school, but my teachers would always say what a great job I did drawing. Then they'd put my drawings on display for everyone to see. That made me feel really good about myself, like I could do something well, like I could do something better than the other kids. That gave me hope.

I think the other thing that drawing did for me was give me some control. I felt like I didn't have any control over my life, but I knew I had control over my drawings.

One day I had the courage to tell my aunt what happened to me. It was really hard, but it felt good to tell someone, and you know, let it out. She told me it wasn't my fault, and she said it was okay. I started to cry; I think I was so relieved. Then she told me it was good to talk about it. She said I shouldn't worry about what people were going to say. She encouraged me to get counseling, even though we both knew my dad didn't like doctors. I think he was afraid of them or maybe just afraid of the truth. But, she knew it would help me.

I have a few male friends now. But mostly I feel more comfortable around my female friends. I'm afraid to let them know what happened, though, because I worry they might not like me if they find out. And when it comes to dating, I'm not sure who I want to ask out, I mean girls my own age or women who are older. I've dated a few girls my own age, but it never feels comfortable. I'm not sure what I'm supposed to do, and I'm afraid to do anything sexual with them. I think

I'm afraid they might hurt me, or I might hurt them.

Counseling has helped. It was great to have someone to talk to. I think the hardest part for me was opening up and telling the doctor what really happened. But, once I told him, it felt good. It also felt good to let go of the anger. I was angry at my dad for the way he treated me and for not being around. I was angry at my mom for drinking, and lying about drinking, and for not protecting me or seeing the signs when I was little. I was angry at my little sister for always blaming me for everything. And, I think I was even angry at myself, like I thought somehow I had done something to deserve it. Anyway, the doctor would bring pillows and foam bats and stuff to my sessions, and he'd let me just get all that anger out. At first it felt weird, but after a while it was fun. And it really helped.

Counseling also helped me to see my own strengths and see my family for what they really are. It helped me see the girls who hurt me differently, too. I know now that what happened to me wasn't my fault. I also know that I didn't do anything to ask for it, and I didn't deserve it, either.

Because of what I've been through, I spent so much time drawing, and got so much out of it, that I'm planning on going to college to become an architect. I think I'll be really good at it.

If I could give advice to parents, I'd say, "Communicate with your kids to develop a trusting bond so that nothing gets hidden. Tell your kids to always feel comfortable with themselves and comfortable to come to you to tell you whatever has happened."

31

I would also tell parents, "Pay attention to little changes, especially anger. If your kids are angry, try to accept it. But most of all try to understand it. That's the way kids show adults something is wrong."

If I could give advice to kids, I'd tell them, "If someone does this to you, it's not your fault. Focus on what you do well. If you can, try to see your abuse as a challenge, then you can use the things you do well to overcome it, and you'll get stronger because of what you've survived."

✸✸✸

As you can see from Lee's story, anyone can be an abuser. It could be a man or a woman, a boy or a girl. It might be a family friend, a stepparent, natural parent, grandparent, aunt or uncle. It could be a babysitter, neighbor, teacher, coach or minister. Or, it might even be a brother or sister, a stepbrother or stepsister, a child you know from school or the neighborhood, or someone you're dating.

Abusers can be rich or poor, well educated or not very educated. They might live in the city, the suburbs or rural areas. And they come from every religious and racial background.

If you walk down a street, you wouldn't be able to pick out a sexual abuser. He or she doesn't look any different or do things openly that are any different from the other people who live around you. If the people who live around you go to work, school or church, the abuser will go, too. If the people who live around you cut their grass, wash their cars or play on the local sports team, the abuser will probably do those things, too. But, privately, when no one else can see, an abuser will develop a slow, trusting relationship with kids and eventually trick or force kids into sexual activity.

Remember: Abusers can be men, women, boys or girls. They don't look any different than anyone else. But, privately, when they are alone with kids, abusers develop slow, trusting relationships that allow them to trick or force kids into sexual activity.

Chapter 3

What Is Sexual Abuse?

Hannah's Story

I had just finished the second grade when it happened to me. I stayed at my grandma's house for the summer. I was seven. My uncle was staying with my grandma then, too, and he and I shared a bedroom because she only had two.

My uncle started out being really nice to me. He took me places and played with me. He even bought me things like ice cream. We had so much fun together. But after a few days, he told me he had a special game he wanted to play with me – only me. He said he picked me because I was special. I liked the way he treated me and I liked the way he made me feel. I trusted him. He was my uncle.

He told me to get undressed and get on the bed. When I did that, he started touching me in my private places. He kissed me there, too, and he made me kiss his privates, too. I didn't like it, but he didn't force me, and he didn't hurt me. I don't really know why I did it, but I did. And whenever I did what he wanted, he bought me something special or took me someplace I really wanted to go, like horseback riding or to the carnival.

One day I told him I didn't want to do it anymore. I said I thought what we were doing was bad. He said he wasn't forcing me. He said I liked it and I wanted him to do it. Then he said it's what married people do. He said he loved me. He said I was his special girl and that he really wanted to marry me. But, if I didn't let him do it to me, he couldn't marry me. Then he told me he'd be very sad if he couldn't marry me. He said he'd be sad if he had to marry someone else. As I was growing up, my mom always said, if I was a good girl, someday a handsome prince would marry me. I always thought that was the most important thing – to have a handsome prince marry me. So I let him keep doing it, even though I really didn't like it, even though I thought what we were doing was wrong. After all, he was right. He wasn't hurting or forcing me. So I guess it was my fault.

I thought about what we did. I wanted to tell my mom, because I felt mixed-up about it. But I couldn't. I promised him I wouldn't tell anyone. But, even if I wanted to tell, I knew I couldn't. My mom and dad were always fighting – I mean fighting so badly that my dad would put his fist through the television or a wall or something, and my mom would throw dishes at my dad, and they'd fight until my mom left for a few days. Then, when she'd come back, they'd make up and be so happy that I just didn't want to say anything. I just wanted everyone to be happy, especially because it was my fault. I let him do it. He didn't force me.

Besides, my mom was always preaching that every time something bad happened to her, it was because she had done something wrong – she always said she deserved it. It kinda scared me when she talked like that. But it really scared me when she said if I was bad, I'd be punished, too, like she was. So, there was no way I could tell her anything.

Anyway, things were different for me after my uncle abused me. I started wetting the bed and having really bad nightmares. I refused to wear dresses and stopped playing with dolls. I wanted to be a boy. I was mad that I was a girl; I was mad about everything. I started fighting with my little sisters, slamming doors, even breaking things when I didn't get my way. I was demanding and bossy with my friends – and pretty soon most kids wouldn't even play with me.

I had an awful time at school, too. I'd daydream all the time. No matter how hard I tried, I just couldn't concentrate. My grades fell, and I remember my mom coming to school one day to talk to my teacher about holding me back. They decided I had a discipline problem and that I should be forced to study harder. So, they put me in the fourth grade.

A few years later, I heard that my uncle had gotten married. When I saw him, I didn't say anything, I just looked at him. But he must have known what I was thinking, because he started telling me he was sure I knew he wasn't really going to marry me. He said he was sure I knew I was too young for him.

Then he said the most awful thing to me. He said he was just practicing on me, you know, so he could be really good when he got married. I know my face turned red, because I was so mad at him I thought I'd burst. I guess he got scared, because he said I better never tell anyone what he did to me – ever. He said if I did, he'd tell my mom I had sinned and she'd punish me.

I was terrified to tell anyone, and devastated that he never really loved me or wanted to marry me. I felt totally betrayed and all alone with my horrible secret. He was my uncle, and I trusted him. I believed him, and he tricked me.

I had my first real love when I was 14. He played on the basketball team, and I was a cheerleader. He was so cute, and he had this thick, wavy black hair – I felt lucky. After the games, he'd take me to the pizza shop, and we'd share a pizza and a Coke. Then he'd walk me home. But it only lasted a few months. He broke up with me. He said he liked someone else. Her name was Julie, and she was prettier than me, more popular and thinner. He walked around school, staring at her, following her, ignoring me, like I wasn't even there – like I had never been there. I felt awful, just like I did when I found out about my uncle.

When I got home from school that day, I ran to my room, slammed the door and broke the little statue that he won for me at the amusement park. I screamed, cried and refused to eat or come out of my room. After dinner, my mom came upstairs and pounded on my door. She said I was acting ridiculous, and she wanted it to stop – right now. She said I had to get over this boy. She said she wouldn't tolerate this temper tantrum any longer. She said my behavior was probably the reason he broke up with me in the first place.

When my mom was downstairs, I came out of my room and shouted to her that I was going to kill myself. I went into the bathroom and locked the door. I took some pills from the medicine cabinet – not enough to kill myself or anything. I guess I just wanted my mother to notice. I guess I just wanted her to help me.

It didn't really matter, though; she didn't take me to the doctor or anything. She just gave me this stuff to make me throw up. She told me that vomiting was my punishment for doing this to myself. It was horrible. I threw up until I didn't think I had anything left inside my skin.

After that, I was terrified of losing any guy who even paid a little bit of attention to me, even the ones who didn't treat me very good. I did whatever I thought I had to do to keep them happy. I didn't care about having girlfriends or going to the mall or sleep-over parties or anything. I only cared about having a boyfriend and keeping him happy. I didn't date a lot of guys or anything, but if I was dating a guy and he wanted sex, I gave him sex – I didn't like it or think it was okay, but I did it just to keep him happy – to keep him the only way I knew how.

I guess all that stuff – the anger, the mixed-up feelings about myself and boys, even the suicide attempt – was because of what my uncle did to me. It was all because I had to grow up with that awful secret inside me – because I had to grow up feeling like it was all my fault.

If I could tell kids something, I'd say, "If anyone is touching you, or did anything to you when you were little, don't believe what he or she says to you. Don't think it's love. That's just what they say to trick you. And don't think it has to hurt to be sexual abuse. If someone has tricked you into doing something sexual, even if they didn't hurt you, it's not your fault. You've been tricked. Talk to someone about what happened, as soon as you can. If you can't talk to your mom or dad, maybe you can talk to an older brother or sister, or a teacher, or a coach, or your best friend's mother – but don't keep it inside you. You have to tell someone what's happened."

✹✹✹

Hannah's story shows that she was mixed-up about what was happening. She loved her uncle and trusted him, and she was confused because her uncle wasn't hurting her. Like Hannah, most kids think touches have to hurt to be abusive. But that's not true. Sexual activities don't have to hurt, and sometimes they even feel good.

Abusers will also try to make you feel comfortable. They'll buy you things, take you places, even tell you you're special or say they love you. That can be very confusing. You might think that if you feel comfortable it's not sexual abuse. But that's not true. Abusers try to make kids feel comfortable so they can trick kids into sexual activity, or keep the sexual activity ongoing.

Sexual abuse happens anytime you are asked, tricked or forced by someone who is bigger, stronger or older than you, or by someone who has some power over you into a sexual activity. They will want you to do secret touching or secret non-touching activities that involve your private parts or the private parts of someone else. You might want to tell, but you know it's a secret; not a fun secret that makes you happy and excited to keep. It's a scary secret, one you are afraid to tell, one that gives you that funny feeling, like butterflies, in your stomach.

There are two main forms of sexual abuse, touching and non-touching. One type of non-touching behavior is when someone shows you movies, pictures or Internet sites with pornography, nude people posing or doing things like having sex. Another type of non-touching behavior happens if someone exposes his or her private body parts to you when you don't want to see them. This is called exhibitionism.

Non-touching behaviors also occur if someone asks you to pose for a picture without clothes or in a sexual way that makes you feel uncomfortable, or if someone takes your picture while you're doing something sexual that doesn't feel comfortable or is confusing. He or she might encourage you to watch or listen to people who are engaging in sexual acts. And, an abuser might also want to watch you undress or bathe.

Sexual harassment is also a form of sexual abuse. Someone might tease you or make you feel uncomfortable about your body or certain clothes you wear, or they might call you bad names. You might be scared to tell on these kids, or you might want them to think you can "take" it. But it's not necessary to put up with their remarks and the uncomfortable way they make you feel. Sexual harassment is abusive, too.

Sexually abusive touching behaviors happen when

someone touches the private parts of your body, over or under your clothes, or makes you touch their body. It also happens if they put any part of their body on or in any part of your body, like their fingers, tongue or private part. Another form of sexually abusive touching occurs if someone puts something that's not a body part – a foreign object – into your body, like soap or the handle of a hairbrush, or crayons.

When someone forces you to have sexual intercourse with them, whether you know that person or not, whether you are on a date with that person or not, that's called rape. Rape also happens if your ability to say "no" is taken away because you are unconscious or drugged. If a date rape drug is slipped into your drink, you won't know what's happening, and you won't be able to protect yourself or say "no" to unwanted sexual advances.

Sometimes adults or doctors may have to touch the private parts of small children – like when changing their diaper, applying medicine or giving them a bath. Adults might need to help older kids, too. If you have a broken arm or leg, for example, you may need help getting in and out of the shower, or you might need help washing. Touching children to keep them clean or healthy is okay, as long as the touching feels comfortable to you. Secret touches, touches that make you feel uncomfortable, are not okay.

Remember: Sexual abuse happens anytime you are asked, tricked or forced by someone who is bigger, stronger or older than you, to do secret touching or secret non-touching that involves your private parts or the private parts of someone else.

Chapter 4

The Internet and You

Faith's Story

My name is Faith and I'm 16. I used to live with my mom, my dad and my little brother. We were pretty close. My parents were our coaches, and we went on vacations all the time. We had a lot of money, and my dad used to buy anything for me. He spoiled me.

When I was 12, things started to change. My dad would have me wear really revealing clothes, and I didn't know why. He encouraged me to do things, like go to the under-21 dance clubs, dressed like that, even though I didn't want to. It just didn't feel right to me, but he was my dad and I did what he wanted.

When we got the Internet, he always encouraged me to go into chat rooms and talk to people and flirt with them, even though I didn't even know who they were. I didn't want to do it, but then, he was my dad, and if I didn't do it, he'd get really mean.

After a few times in the chat rooms, I just didn't feel comfortable, so I stopped e-mailing and responding to their e-mails. But they kept sending me e-mails saying things like "thanks for the reply," or "thanks for the pictures." But I didn't send any pictures and I didn't know what was going on.

One day this guy started pursuing and threatening me. He told me I had to send him specific pictures – like a picture of me with a man putting his finger inside me, or a picture with a man ejaculating on my stomach. He said if I didn't send him those pictures, he was going to post the naked pictures he had of me all over the Internet and send them to all my friends at school.

I really didn't know how to approach it because you can't find out who anybody is on the Net. Anytime I'd try to search for him, he'd send me a nasty e-mail saying, "Don't try to find me."

So, I went to my dad and asked him to block this guy's e-mail address. He said he called the Internet place and had it blocked, but the guy must have signed up for a new name. Well, I called the Internet place myself, and the person there said it was never blocked. So I blocked it, but this guy just got a new name. I called the company again, and they said they really couldn't do anything about it. So, I went to my dad again, but he said he thought it would be best if I just posed for the pictures. That's when I got really suspicious.

My dad was always walking around the house with a digital camera in his hand. He'd take pictures of everything. He took pictures of my mom in the kitchen and my brother. I think he did that so he wouldn't seem suspicious. But mostly he took pictures of me. He'd walk in on me, in my bedroom and in the bathroom, like I'd be stepping out of the shower, and he'd take my picture. If I said something to him, he'd say, "Oh, don't worry, I'm going to erase it," and stuff like that.

After my dad left for work one day, I started looking around on the desk and in the computer, trying to figure out what was going on. I found naked pictures of me in the shower, getting out of the shower and stuff. My dad wasn't erasing those pictures. He was sending them to people I didn't know. He betrayed me the whole time. He lied to me.

When I approached him on it and threatened to tell my mom, he got really angry. He said if I told her, she'd hate me. He said it would ruin their marriage. He said she loved him and she'd forgive him, but she'd never forgive me. Then he said I had to take the pictures the e-mail guy demanded. He said I had to take them with him. He told me if I didn't do what he wanted, I wouldn't be allowed to do anything. He grabbed my face and squeezed it. I knew if I didn't do what he wanted, he'd hurt me. He was really angry and really strong. He scared me, so I did it because I didn't have a choice. It made me sick.

For over a year, my dad took pictures of me. He photographed the two of us doing sexual things. Then he'd send them all over the Internet. He even built a website and posted my pictures there. I saw his website once, but when I went back to look for it again, when I tried to find the pictures on our computer, everything was gone. The proof was gone and I didn't know how to stop him.

I didn't have anyone to talk to. I had lost most of my

friends because my dad wouldn't let me hang out with them. He'd only let me hang out with guys. I wasn't allowed to have any girlfriends at all. If I started getting too close to somebody, I wouldn't be allowed to hang out with them. I used to be close to my grandma, but my dad wouldn't let me stay at her house anymore, either. I was just really far away from everybody. I was so isolated and scared. It was awful.

Most of all, I wanted to talk to my mom, but I felt mixed-up. I didn't have any proof, and I didn't think she'd believe me without it. Besides, he was her husband and I wasn't close to her anymore. He wouldn't let me spend any time alone with her. It was always him and me. And I was always fighting with her, and treating her and my little brother really mean. And there was also my little brother. He idolized my dad, he was his baseball coach – everything. It just didn't seem fair of me to tell. I felt like, if I protected myself, I'd just hurt everyone else. So I stayed quiet.

I felt like my life was just turned upside down, like it was totally wrong. When I was younger, my dad was my life. My parents didn't get married until I was five, and all I ever wanted was for them to get married so I could be with him. And then, for him to betray me and do something like that – it just hurt me so bad. I guess that's why it was so hard for me.

I had all this hatred inside me, and the longer things went on, the worse it got. I was really mean to my mom, and I beat up on my younger brother all the time. I don't know why. I guess I just wanted my mom to know that something was wrong. I don't know, I think maybe I was hoping, since I couldn't tell her, that maybe she'd ask.

I really wanted to be close to her, I mean, she was my mom, and we had this awesome relationship before everything started. Then it all fell apart. I couldn't talk to her and she thought I was shutting her out of my life. Then he'd tell her I was the one who wanted to wear these revealing clothes. I know she was disappointed, especially since I was only 12 years old. She didn't understand why I only hung out with guys, either – she didn't think it was right, and I know she didn't like it.

Sometimes I'd just sit there, look at her and think "please, please understand." But I didn't say anything to her because I was so afraid of him, because I was afraid of hurting her, and because I was afraid she wouldn't believe me. It was so hard. I felt trapped and isolated, like it would be better if I just killed myself. I cut my wrists and, sometimes, I'd burn myself with a lighter. Sometimes, I even thought about killing him. But even though I was lashing out at everyone, and hurting myself, no one asked if I was all right.

One morning, I got up early and my dad was typing an e-mail. I happened to glance at it and recognized a few words that were in the e-mail – the threatening e-mail from that guy. That's when I realized it was my dad sending those threatening e-mails to me. He was doing it so he could keep taking my picture. I felt horrible, sick. I checked the computer, looking for proof, but everything was gone. He had erased it all. I felt trapped. He was supposed to be my dad. He was supposed to be protecting me from stuff like that, but he was pushing me into it.

The next day, I was putting away my dad's clean T-shirts

in his dresser drawer, when I found all these floppy disks with my name on them. I put the disks in the computer and opened them, and it was me, nude, getting out of the shower, stuff like that. They said things like "Faith nude" or "Faith getting out of the shower."

After I found the disks, I knew. I mean before, it was just going to be my word against his, and I was afraid my mom wasn't going to believe me. But now that I had the proof to show her, I wasn't so afraid.

As soon as she came home from work that day, I showed them to her. She was really upset with my dad, and really supportive of me. She told me how sorry she was for what I had been going through. She said she was sorry she didn't realize, and didn't help me. All those things I worried about didn't happen. She did believe me, and she did stick by me, not him.

My mom didn't know what to do. She didn't want to just take the disks and have him come home from work and know something was up, because he could get pretty mean, and then he might just get rid of the evidence. So, right away, she called her friend, Shelly, who is a police officer. She asked Shelly what to do.

Shelly came over the next day, while he was at work. But he came home on his lunch hour and saw Shelly there. I think he suspected something. My mom left the disks in his drawer, so he wouldn't think we were doing anything. But that night, while they were at my brother's football practice, my parents got into a fight. When they got home, my dad hid the disks.

I was really scared after that, because I had already contacted the police and I had already talked to Child Protective Services, and now the proof was gone. Without the disks, I didn't think anyone was going to believe me.

But my mom was determined to protect me, and while my dad was at work, she and I searched the house. We found the disks in the attic. We called Shelly right away, and when he came home that day on his lunch break, he was arrested.

I wasn't home when the police came. I was with my mom and Shelly at her house. They took me there so he couldn't hurt me. That night I didn't go home. I didn't want to. I stayed with my grandma because I was still scared, even though I knew he had been arrested.

I guess everyone gets through difficult times in different ways. For me, I didn't have many friends, and I didn't have anything else to do, so I put my entire time into softball and my school work. I never missed softball practice and usually stayed later than I had to. Softball gave me a positive way to release some of my anger. And because I never wanted to be home, I was always at school. When classes were over, I'd stay in the library and study. I kept up a 4.0 grade point average and still keep a 3.8 to 4.0 today.

I think even though this has been really hard, it's made me stronger, and it has made my relationship with my mom better. It's also made me a better big sister. I'm really protective of my little brother. Now, I watch out for him, instead of beating him up. I also think it's given me some direction, too. Before, I wasn't sure what I wanted to study in college, but now I know I want to go into psychology. I want to help people going through what I've been through.

I think one of the reasons I'm doing so well now is because of counseling. When I first went, I didn't open up. I kept the stress of everything deep inside me. One day, my blood pressure started to drop, and I passed out. I woke up in the hospital. That's when I realized I couldn't just go to counseling and sit there. I had to open up and let this stuff out.

Since then, things have really gone well. My counselor is terrific, and she has helped me to know it wasn't my fault. She helped me realize I didn't do anything to deserve what he did. And even though it was my dad, he didn't single me out or anything. What happened to me could have happened to anybody, and maybe he was doing it to other kids, too. I don't know. I don't want to know.

After two years of counseling sessions, the counselor said I'm doing really well, and I'm done. I had to promise her I'd call if I needed her. I think she already knew I would.

Now, things with my mom are just great. Even though we lost our house, had to move, and my mom had to go back to work, she's been there for me every step of the way. I know I can tell her anything. I know I can count on her. I also know she feels guilty because she didn't see it, but I keep telling her it wasn't her fault. I keep telling her that counseling helped me, and she should go, too, so she doesn't have to feel that way anymore.

If I could give advice to kids, I'd say, "If you're going on the Internet, be smart about it. If you want to talk to your friends, use instant messaging, only e-mail people you know, and never go into chat rooms." I'd also tell them, "The Internet isn't a safe way to meet people. You have no way of knowing if the person you're talking to is who they say they are. I mean, you might think you're talking to a 12-year-old boy, when you're really talking to a 65-year-old man. It's just not safe. Definitely, never give out any information about yourself, not even your cell phone number. Strangers can connect any little bit of information to you, and if they want to, they'll find you."

I'd like to tell adults, "Pay attention to the little things. Look deep. Read between the lines. Just because your kid is out there doing something or dressing some way, doesn't mean he or she wants to. But, if you find out something has happened, be supportive and help your kid, but don't feel guilty. It's not your fault."

❊ ❊ ❊

The Internet is an exciting place to go to learn new things and explore new places. But as Faith quickly learned, it's also a dangerous place. People who want to take advantage of kids will pose as children in chat rooms. You have no way of knowing if the person you meet in a chat room is who they say they are. They might not be someone you can trust. They might be someone who wants to trick you into sexual activity.

NEVER *use the Internet to meet new people.*

NEVER *give out any personal information over the Internet. Don't tell anyone your age, your address, your birth date, the name of your school, your home phone number or your cell phone number. Even the smallest amount of information can help an abuser find you.*

NEVER *arrange a face-to-face meeting with someone you've met on the Internet. If they want to meet you, tell someone right away.*

NEVER *open links in e-mails from people you don't know.*

NEVER *respond to messages that are sexual in any way. Tell someone right away if someone sends you pornography, talks to you about sex, or tries to convince you to go along with any type of touching or non-touching sexual activity.*

Remember: The Internet can be an exciting place to learn new things and explore new places. But, it is a dangerous place, too. Abusers use the Internet to find kids they can trick or force into sexual activity.

Chapter 5

I Can Take Care of Myself

Alysha's Story

I'm a 17-year-old high school junior. I'm a private person. I don't have many friends, but the people who are my friends are nice. I love to play basketball. That's my main focus right now, playing basketball. I love singing and dancing, and making flower arrangements. And, I love to have fun. But it wasn't always like that for me.

The stuff that I was doing was a reaction to what I was feeling about my mom, about my dad, and how my sister and I weren't getting along. I did stuff that I shouldn't have done, you know, trying to be a grown-up or just trying to play adult roles that were not really me.

My dad wasn't really around all the time, but when he was, it was cool. My mom used to always be there for us, but then she started fading away and stopped coming home. We hadn't seen our mom for a long, long time. I was only six or seven then, and my sister was about 11. She and I used to be home all alone. The door didn't have a lock on it so we used to have to put a chair against it. Our house was cold because we only had one small space heater, and we didn't have any food. There were only cans of tomato soup there. My sister would go to the store and steal food, just so we could eat. We had to do everything for ourselves, even wake ourselves up for school.

One day Child Protective Services came to school and took my sister and me away. They made us move in with my aunt and uncle. I didn't want to go there. I knew it wasn't going to be good.

I was right. That's when all heck broke loose. No matter what I did, either no one paid any attention to me or I was getting beat. One time a teacher called about me and when I got home, I got a beating. The teachers used to call my aunt about my cousin all the time, but did he get punished – no. One time I went next door to my other aunt's to get some bread to make a sandwich, and when I got back, my uncle slapped me in the face. I don't even know what I did. He never told me.

I felt like I was the black sheep of the family. Nothing I did was right. No one cared about me or how I was feeling. They wanted me to listen to them, but they wouldn't listen to me. They wanted me to respect them, but they wouldn't respect me.

I think it would have helped if my aunt would have talked to me when I first went to her house. But she didn't work with me. I was just taken out of my house, taken away from my mom. My mom was my heart, and when she was gone, my heart was broken. My aunt didn't ask me how I was feeling or what I needed to get through this, or what she could do to make me feel comfortable in her house. She didn't do anything. So I thought, "You're not doing anything for me, so why should I do anything for you?"

I thought nobody cared about me, so I didn't care either. I thought, I know I'm young, but no one here is going to take care of me, so I've got to do things for myself. Even though my sister was there, I felt like I had to take care of myself. I felt like I had to grow up. So I grew up too fast.

I didn't respect adults. I did stuff just to fit in, basically. I wore tight, short clothes just to get attention. I thought I had all the answers, and even if someone tried to tell me something, I didn't listen, because I thought I had it all figured out. I thought I was in control. I thought everything was all about me and I just wanted to do whatever I wanted to do.

Right away I started liking boys. When I was just eight I used to play hide-and-go-get-it, doctor and stuff like that. By the time I was 11, I was getting into stuff like drugs and cigarettes. Even though I wasn't having sex, yet, I was doing stuff with boys, like grinding, heavy kissing, playing spin the bottle – stuff like that.

By the time I was 14, I was really doing a lot of things I shouldn't have. I was trying to be a grown-up and trying to find someone to love me, to buy me things and take care of me, because I didn't have anyone doing that for me. That's when I got involved with older men.

I saw this older man in a church. He was 35. He was supposed to be a Christian, and he had his Bible under his arm. I saw him; and when I wanted something I'd go after it, so I started looking at him and saying stuff to him. But I realized he wasn't really paying attention to me. So I went deeper. I wanted to know why he wasn't paying attention to me.

He said things like, "Oh, I like you, but you're young. If you were older then I'd really mess with you." I thought, why would he say that – he was already trying to talk to me. So we started hanging out. Then, one day, we were driving around, and he took me to a park. He started to get close. He started kissing and touching me. Then he came over to my seat. I knew he wanted to have sex with me. I mean he didn't really force me, but I didn't really have a choice because I wanted him to want to be with me. So I did it. After that, I just felt low. I felt that he just thought of me differently.

The next day he wouldn't speak to me. He hung out with his other friends, and just looked at me as if to say, "Okay, she's easy and I know how she is now, so I'm not going to pay any attention to her." And I thought, "What happened? Did you forget about last night?"

Later that night, I went over to a party at this guy's house and he was there. He came over to me and he was trying to be all close and sweet talk me. And I thought that maybe I could still get him to want me. So, we had sex upstairs in this guy's house. And, after, I felt bad. I felt used. I felt like he only wanted me for one thing. Even though he wasn't really pressuring me out loud to do it, he really was, because he wasn't asking me how I felt. He wasn't asking me if I really wanted to do it. He just did it to me.

When I saw him again, we went for a ride in his car, and

he said he had to let me go. He said, "If you were older, then I'd talk to you because I really like you, but being that you're young, I can't." And I thought, "Why would you say that now, after you had sex with me, after you took something that was valuable to me?" It was like he was saying I did what I had to do and I'm done with you. I felt used, and I really felt bad about myself. I was angry all the time. I walked around without a smile. I was always mad, even if nobody did anything to me that day. I couldn't open myself up, even when people were trying to help me.

I had good grades up until that point in my life. I started failing, and I was about to drop out of school. I didn't want to do it anymore. I didn't think anyone cared about me. I'd look in the mirror and think "you're not special." I thought I was ugly. I thought I was nothing, stupid, just nothing. And I wanted to die. I couldn't do it anymore. I couldn't stay at my aunt's house anymore. And I couldn't think about what he did to me, either. That's when I ran away.

I had run away before, but this time when I went to school, Child Protective Services was there, waiting for me. My aunt had never done that before, and this time she put me in a shelter. I guess she just thought that living with her wasn't any good for me, so maybe it would be better for me in the shelter. I guess it was, because that's when I knew I had to change. That's when I wanted to change.

I wanted to stop being who I was. I wanted to stop hurting for my mom. I wanted to stop crying every night, praying that I'd find a new home. I wanted to be free. I was tired of being in bondage, trapped by the stuff I was surrounded by. I wanted to be out of it. I was searching for someone to love me for who I was. I was trying to find myself, to see who I was, because what I was doing wasn't me. I didn't know myself, and even though I was accepting it, other people were telling me that wasn't me.

I started going to church, praying and talking to other people about finding myself and changing. I never went to counseling – professional counseling – but I had a lot of adults around me who listened. They made me notice that life's not always bad. God wouldn't give me more than I could bear. They told me there's always a way out. They helped me see that I had a choice – I could either make it better or make it worse.

Changing isn't about what other people do for you. It's about what you want to do for yourself. It's about whether you really want to be a better person or not, and I really wanted it. So I did it. I changed. And I guess God was trying to tell me something, too. He was trying to make me see things for what they were and stop trying to use my mom as an excuse for doing what I was doing – just plain old "acting out" – just going crazy for no reason when I didn't have to, when I had another choice.

I think because of what I've been through I'm stronger. I know that if I made it through this, I can make it through anything. I'm more focused now, too. I'm seeing things as I should see them. Instead of leaning to my own understanding of what the situation may be, I'm starting to see things as outsiders see them, looking in. And I want to listen to the opinions of others, even when it hurts, I know they are just trying to help me. I know that when you do something out of character that hurts your body, or hurts someone else, that's abuse. I know that I wasn't as grown-up as I thought, and I know that I shouldn't have been with older men. I now know that they were taking advantage of me. They were just using me. And I know that even though I thought I was in control, I really wasn't. Kids can't do it on their own. They need help.

If I was going to give advice to kids, I'd say, "If you feel like something's not right, or if you just aren't sure, then don't do it. If you don't know what to do or where to get help, go to church and get into God. That's the love that everybody's looking for. That's the love you need to make a change in your life." I'd also tell kids, "Don't have sex, or drink, or do things out of anger, because then you'll only be in another bad situation. Always believe in yourself and always know yourself. And no matter what you're going through, try to keep your head up and remember that even though you think you're the only one going through something, you're not. Other people out there are going through hard stuff, too."

I'd tell kids, "If you don't understand something, take notes. Write it down and go to someone you feel you can trust, and talk about it. People are getting hurt, raped and abused, and they think it's their fault. They think it's because of something they did. But it's not, and they don't know that."

If I could give advice to parents, I'd say, "Be there more. Always know your kids' friends, know where they're going and know what they're doing. Always pay attention to everything. Talk to them about everything – don't be harsh, just talk to them. Don't be scared to talk to them about the hard stuff, like sex and drugs. And always recognize the good things in your kids, before your recognize the bad. Never put your kids down, because that's where it starts – in the home. If you put your kids down long enough, they'll believe it."

I'd also tell parents, "Don't let your problems make you forget about your kids. Don't do drugs or run off with someone and forget about your kids. Your kids see everything you're doing. They don't miss anything. Think about your kids first, in every situation."

✹✹✹

Like Alysha, you might think you can take care of yourself. You might think you're grown-up and in control. You might think you can handle things on your own.

Alysha was lucky because her abuser ended the relationship with her. But, if you try to resist or end the relationship with your abuser, you might not be so lucky. The abuser might get angry and yell at you. He or she might hit you, or scare you, or say something like, "I'm the only one who really loves you." Or, he or she might tell you, "I'll hurt your little brother or sister (or someone else close to you), if you tell anyone." Or, "You owe me this for all the nice things I've done for you."

The abuser might also try to convince you it was your fault. He or she might say, "You made me do it," or "You flirted with me," or "When you danced in front of me, I just couldn't help myself," or "You liked it. You wanted it. It's your fault."

The abuser might also convince you that if you tell, you won't be believed. He or she might say, "Go ahead, tell someone. They won't believe you. You don't have any proof." Or the abuser might say, "If your mom (or dad, or the teacher) has to choose between you and me, he or she will pick me. So you better keep your mouth shut."

You might stay quiet because you feel guilty or scared, or you might stay quiet because you think you can handle things on your own. If the person abusing you is someone you know from school or your school bus, you might want them to think you can take it. You might be afraid of what they will say or what other kids will think if you tell. But as Alysha found out, kids can't protect themselves from sexual abusers. Kids need trusting adults to keep them safe.

Remember: Kids cannot protect themselves from sexual abusers. Abusers are usually bigger, stronger, older or in charge of you. They will trick and threaten you into staying quiet so the sexual abuse can happen or continue. In order to get safe, and stay safe, you need to tell a trusting adult as soon as you can.

Chapter 6

What to Do if You're Approached

Jill's Story

I was ten years old when my friends' father molested me. It was May 31. I'll never forget that day. My friends and I were playing. We had dinner at my house, and then I invited them to sleep over, only we had to wait until their father came home to ask permission. Once he came home, we went to their house to ask. My friends were not allowed to stay at my house, but I was allowed to stay at theirs. At first, my parents refused, because they said it just wasn't right, you know, that I could stay at their house, but they couldn't stay at mine. But we all begged my parents, and finally they gave in and said I could stay overnight.

After we were told to go to bed, my friends' father came upstairs and kept flicking the hall lights. He would turn the lights on and come into the room where I was sleeping and stare at me. I didn't really like it, but I wasn't too scared at first. But when he kept doing it, I was wondering what was going on. There was a storm that night, and between my friends' father playing with the lights and the thunder and lightening, I had trouble sleeping.

I knew it was getting late because I was really tired, and I closed my eyes and tried very hard to sleep. I was with my friend in her double bed when he came into the room again. I pretended to be asleep, but I could hear him beside me. I peeked and saw him removing his boxer shorts. He was standing beside the bed without any clothes on. He was naked, and he was scaring me. I didn't know what to do.

He grabbed my hand and made me touch him. I pulled my hand away with all my strength, and he grabbed it again. I tried to pull away again, but he was too strong for me. He held my wrist real tight and made me touch him and rub him. While he was making me touch him, he used his other hand to try and open my mouth. He put his fingers in my mouth and held it open and leaned toward my face. I was so afraid. I wanted him to stop, and with all my might, I pulled away from him and rolled over.

He left the room and I started to cry. I wanted my mother. I woke up my friend and said I wanted to go home. She took me to her older sister's room. Her dad was in there, in the bed with her sister. She asked if I could call my mom. He wanted to know why, and I lied and told him I forgot to tell my mom something really important. I told him my stomach was hurting.

At first he didn't want me to call her. He said I'd be okay and I should just go back to bed. But I told him I needed to call her because I wasn't going to be okay. I started to cry, so he said I could call her.

I knew my mom was scared when I called, because I had never done that before. I had been to lots of sleepovers, but this was the first time I ever went home in the middle of the night. We only lived two doors down, and my mom said she would wait for me in the garage. When I got outside, it was really dark and raining hard with a lot of thunder and lightening. I was so scared that he was going to follow me that I ran all the way to my house, yelling that something bad happened. I cried out that he hurt me.

When I got home, I was afraid to tell my mom what happened because I didn't know what my friends' father would do to me if I told. My mom said I was safe in my house and that no one was going to hurt me. She told me that she and my dad would protect me from him. That's when I told her what happened.

I had to tell my story to three policemen in the hospital, the District Attorney and other important people. They said I couldn't even talk to my mom or dad about what happened. So whenever I thought about it, I just cried a lot and told my mom I'm thinking about "you know," but I couldn't talk about it because they said I wasn't allowed.

I thought those kids were my friends, but after I told on their father they wouldn't talk to me anymore, and when they did, they said mean things to me. They were mad at me for telling. They blamed me because they had to move away. They said it was my fault, and they did mean things to me.

Even after they moved, I still got really scared and would make my mom lock all the doors and windows and pull the drapes closed so no one could look in. We finally got a security system, and even when my mom would turn it on and lock us inside, I still didn't feel safe. I kept thinking he might come after me for telling, or just want to do it again.

I didn't know why he did it to me. I didn't know why he hated me so much. I never did anything to hurt him or his kids. Why did he pick me? I couldn't sleep very well, and my mom had to stay with me at night until I fell asleep. I loved my dad and knew he protected me, but I couldn't give him a hug or a kiss because he was a man, and a man hurt me.

It's been two years since it happened to me, and my mom and dad moved us to a new state. They thought it might help me feel safer, but I'm still afraid. I don't feel like I can trust anyone. I don't feel like I know who my friends are, so I spend most of my time with my family and at gymnastics, but not with my friends. I just don't feel like I can trust anyone, even kids.

There are still nights when I see shadows and need my mom to hold me until I fall asleep, but at least I feel safe with her. I'm starting to feel safe with my dad, too. I can even give him a hug sometimes. With counseling, I'm learning the difference between the person who hurt me and my dad and other trusting men in my life.

I just want all of this to go away. I don't want to have to think about it anymore, or be afraid anymore. I don't know how long it will take for me to feel better, but I want to feel better so bad.

I used to be really outgoing, and it was easy for me to trust people, and making friends was what I did best. Now things are different. I get along with people okay, but I don't want anyone to get too close or get to know me too much. I decide who I want to talk to, and who I don't. I stay close to home now, where I feel safe.

I know my mom, dad and brother love me. But sometimes I get really mad at them, even when they didn't do anything. My counselor told me it's good to use some of my anger when I practice gymnastics. My gymnastics teacher said it seems like I do a lot better at the hard stuff if I'm upset. Everyone keeps telling me gymnastics is a good way to use bad feelings. I don't think I really understand all that stuff, but it feels good to get the bad feelings out, and I'm lucky to be good at gymnastics.

I'll be starting cheerleading in a few weeks, and when I'm not at cheerleading practice or gymnastics, I study hard, because it's really important that I'm good in school, so I can be a doctor when I grow up.

If I could talk to kids, I'd say, "If someone tries to touch you, get away from them as soon as you can, and tell someone, right away. Your body belongs to you. No one should ever touch you in a *secret* way – no one."

✳ ✳ ✳

Jill was very frightened about what happened to her, but she was able to get away from her friends' father before anything more happened to her. She was smart, too. She knew how important it was to tell someone, right away.

If you are forced into secret touching or secret non-touching activities, you might not be able to protect yourself from your abuser. If you are tricked, you might not realize what's happening until after you've been abused. Then, when you do realize what has happened, you might feel guilty, ashamed or responsible. You might be afraid that if you tell, you'll be blamed, punished or not believed.

But whether the abuser tricked or forced you into secret sexual activities doesn't matter. Either way, it's sexual abuse. And sexual abuse is never the child's fault. As soon as you are in a safe place, with an adult you trust, tell the adult what has happened, so he or she can help you get safe and stay safe.

Remember: Anytime you are tricked or forced into sexual activity, it's never your fault. Tell a trusting adult as soon as you can. It's the only way to get safe and stay safe.

Chapter 7

My Best Friend Just Told Me Something

Elizabeth's Story

Julie and I had been friends with Christine for a couple months when we noticed a change in her. She used to be really happy and then suddenly she seemed really sad. When Julie and I asked her if she was okay, she wrote a note, and during class passed it to us, saying we both should read it. The note said that Christine had been hurt, sexually, by one of her older friends – a college boy who was a friend of the family.

Christine was very tall and pretty, and she looked older than she was. So, it didn't surprise us that this boy would like her. She said he really hurt her, he wouldn't leave her alone, and he touched her in places she didn't want to be touched. She was very upset by it.

Julie and I promised her that we would be her friends, stick by her and that she could trust us. She made us promise that we couldn't tell; we could never, ever tell. She said it would get worse if we told, and she wouldn't be our friend anymore. That really made us feel strange, because we had been such good friends with her, and we didn't want to lose her as a friend. We really wanted to help her.

At first, we didn't know what to do, so we didn't tell anyone. We did some research on what we could do to help Christine. We looked in the phone book and got on-line to find some numbers she could call. We wrote down phone numbers and places she could go. And we made a list of people she could talk to.

Julie and I put the information on note cards and gave it to her. We thought if we weren't allowed to help by telling anyone, then she would have to help herself by calling someone. But she threw the cards away. We were really confused about why she would do that. And we were really upset because we tried our hardest to help her. We felt like she expected so much of us, wanting us to help, but not letting us tell anyone. We were also very worried about her. We knew that she was not safe and that the abuse was still going on. We said, "Why don't you tell your mom," and she said that she couldn't tell her because she wouldn't believe her. She also said she couldn't tell her because he was a family friend.

A little while later Christine told us she was pregnant. We were really upset. We thought, well you wouldn't let us help you. Then she started talking about getting an abortion and other stuff that was just really scary because we weren't allowed to tell anyone.

We didn't know what to do. Finally, we sat down with Christine and said we needed to tell someone. We said we can't do this. It won't work. But, she still said that we couldn't tell anyone or she wouldn't trust us anymore, and she wouldn't be our friend anymore. She also said that if we told, we wouldn't be helping her. So we let it go. We did as much as we could for Christine; we were there for her.

Then, she started talking about how she was going to kill herself, and how suicidal she felt. And that was when we drew the line. We knew if she hurt herself, we would blame ourselves, because we didn't do anything when we could have.

So I decided to talk to my mom. My mom runs a clinic. She knows a lot about this stuff, and she helps lots of kids. I explained to her what was going on. I asked her what I should do. She was very helpful about it, and said that she could talk to Christine. But Christine wouldn't talk to her, and she wouldn't do any of the stuff we suggested. She didn't want to get help. Julie and I decided she was afraid, so we would go to a teacher.

There was a female teacher who was really good with us. She was young and understood us, and I was pretty close with her. Julie and I went to her, and told her that we didn't know what to do about Christine. We told her we were really scared, because Christine was suicidal and getting worse every day. At school, we had a program where, if a teacher finds out that a student is thinking about suicide, the teacher goes to other people in the program, and they talk about what to do to prevent it. After meeting with the people in the suicide program, she did what we were the most afraid of. She called Christine's mom.

Christine was very upset with Julie and me. When she

came to school the next day, she said we had ruined her life. She said we messed up everything and everything was going wrong, and now she was going to have an abortion. It was all our fault. She said her mom and dad had hit her, and she went on and on about how awful it was and how it was all our fault. I felt so horrible. Julie and I didn't know how to feel or what to think.

Things with Christine kept getting worse. She started writing stories about what was going on, and how Julie and I had messed up her life. The notes got worse and worse, and it kept on going until the principal got involved. She said we had to stop reading Christine's notes, and we had to meet with her and tell her what was going on, so she could help Christine.

We were willing to meet with the principal because we really wanted to help Christine. It was really scary, because we didn't know how to help, but we figured if we did the right thing, eventually she wouldn't be mad at us anymore. After we told the principal, Christine started changing her story. I mean, she wasn't making sense, like she'd say one thing one day and something different the next day.

Julie and I started to think she was lying to us. We weren't mad, but we were upset because we had done so much and we weren't allowed to tell anyone, and it kept getting worse. We asked her if she was lying, because her story changed every day. But she said she wasn't lying. She said she'd never lie about something like that. She said no one would ever lie about it. But it got to the point where her story was just not believable anymore.

We told her we thought she was lying, and we said that we didn't really believe her anymore. That's when she said she was going to kill us. We were really scared. There was a big meeting with the principal and her parents, who agreed to put her into counseling.

I'm not sure if she was really abused this time, but she told Julie and me that she had been abused a couple of years ago, when she was 11. I think that part was true. I think she was really afraid no one would believe her now. And I think she was trying to live with it like it didn't happen. But now that she was 14, it was just in her head, and she couldn't live with it anymore. I think she really needed someone to know what happened to her. Maybe she needed someone to help her get it all out of her head. Maybe she didn't know how else to do it.

This whole thing was so difficult for Julie and me because we didn't know what to think or what to do, especially when we couldn't tell someone. But, we really think we did our best to help her, even if she doesn't want to be our friend anymore. I know Christine went to a clinic, like my mom's, where she was evaluated and got some help. The counselors helped her understand that it was over, she was safe and she could let go of it. They helped her know she could go on with her life and not live in the past. I know that Julie and I were able to help Christine, even if we lost her friendship, because now she's more like her old self. She's happy again, like she used to be. She's making friends and getting involved in school again.

I think kids are so afraid to tell someone about abuse

because in friendship, trust is the most important thing. If friends tell you a secret about someone they have a crush on, or little things like that, you're expected not to tell. If you do tell, you'll lose a friend and their trust. And that can feel even worse.

Even if a friend tells you something bad, like about abuse, the trust expectancy is still there. It's a commitment that you have to make. It's so hard with friendships, having to keep secrets and promises. If you tell them, it's the worst thing in the world. But, if it's an important secret, like child abuse or suicide, and you don't tell, then you'll regret it later, if something bad happens.

My biggest advice for kids would be, "Think about what will happen if you don't tell. Don't be scared to tell, because it will only get better if you get help for someone. Even if telling costs you that friendship, it is still worth it, because you know you were the real true friend. And, probably, the person will forgive you when they get help."

✳ ✳ ✳

Child abuse is a scary secret and sometimes it's easier to tell a friend, rather than an adult. If your friend has told you a scary secret, you might be feeling mixed-up about what has happened to your friend and chances are, you won't know what to do. You might want to tell someone, but you might feel like you have to keep your friend's secret, especially if you promised not to tell. But as long as you or your friend keeps the scary secret, no one is safe.

Children cannot protect themselves from sexual abusers. Kids need the help of trusting adults to get safe and stay safe. If your friend doesn't want to tell an adult by him or herself, maybe you can go along. Maybe he or she will even want you to tell someone for him or her.

But even if your friend doesn't want anyone to know his or her secret, even if you've promised not to tell, even if you think you might lose that friend, remember that as long as you keep your friend's secret, he or she could be hurt again, and other kids could be hurt, too. In order to help your friend get safe, tell an adult what has happened.

Remember: Even if your friend doesn't want you to tell, even if you promised to keep his or her secret, even if you might risk losing that friend, in order to help your friend get safe, you need to tell his or her scary secret.

Chapter 8

Talking Is a Great Way to Stay Safe

Phillip's Story

The physical abuse started after both my parents died. I was ten. I moved in with my uncle. At the time, I didn't know he was a crack-head. But as time went on, it showed itself to me. When I was living with him, it seemed like I was always doing something wrong, but I never actually did anything wrong. Still, he'd get mad about something. I didn't always know why, and he'd hit me with just about anything – cords, chairs, pieces of wood – just about anything he could get his hands on. It made me feel like I was always wrong, and I thought all the things other people did were my problem – my fault.

After a while I just couldn't take the beating anymore so I moved to Virginia to live with my cousin. Everything there was okay, but I was homesick. So I moved back to Philadelphia to live with another uncle. I was maybe about 12 then. In that household, there was just my uncle and his wife. She was his second wife, and I didn't know her that well. Besides, she was always working and wasn't home much. That left me alone with my uncle a lot.

I wasn't there long when this uncle started beating me, too. But, this time it was worse in a sense, because I was out of the situation when I was in Virginia, and now it came right back into my life. It was even worse for me because I didn't know my first uncle that well, and I'd distance myself from him when he'd get mean and hit me. But I knew this uncle really well. I was good friends with his son, and I'd visit them, so I trusted him and I wanted to be with him. I never thought he'd do anything to me. But when he was drinking, the alcohol just seemed to take control of him.

When he'd beat me, I'd seclude myself from everyone. I'd run to my room to be by myself. I didn't even want to be part of the family or eat with them or anything. I just wanted to practice my music. I just wanted to be alone.

One day my uncle hurt me really bad and I went to my cousin's house for comfort; he was 22. I wanted him to help me, or find a way to make it stop. I started telling him how my uncle was beating me and punching me. He started hugging me, trying to comfort me. I thought he wanted to help me. But then he started touching me and I was thinking, "What is this?" He touched my leg and then he tried to touch my private part. I knew right away what he was doing, and I knew it wasn't right.

I knew what he was doing because before my mother died, she told me she had been sexually abused as a child. She would always tell me "Watch out! Watch out!" because it can be the person you least suspect. I didn't really take it in, but my real brothers would say, "You better listen because it might happen to you, and you might not know what to do and you'll be stuck." Because of what my mother and brothers taught me, and because I knew I shouldn't let anyone do that to me, I protected myself.

I had always been a big guy all my life, and my cousin was really skinny. So I tried to intimidate him and hide my fear, but I was really afraid. I didn't know what he was going to do. He was a lot older than me, and even though he wasn't very big, he was probably a lot stronger. I tried to intimidate him with my size and weight and luckily I was able to stop anything from happening to me. I couldn't believe it happened to me. I always liked and respected him as a person. But at that moment my respect for him disappeared.

Because of my age, I was more comfortable telling my other cousins rather than my aunt. When I told them, they didn't know what to do. My cousins kept saying stuff like, "I just can't believe he'd do that." It wasn't that they didn't believe me, it was just that they couldn't believe he'd do something like that, especially when they knew I went to him for comfort after my uncle hurt me. I don't know if they ever confronted my cousin, and I always wondered if he ever did it to anyone else. But, I didn't see him after that for a long time, because that's when the police came and I was put into a foster home because of what my uncle did to me.

I know because of everything that happened to me, I have trouble trusting people. I have trouble being around people and having associations with people for a long period of time, especially my family. But some good has come out of all of it, too. I mean, I have my music. If I hadn't been abused, I probably wouldn't have turned to music for comfort. I probably wouldn't have practiced so much. And, I think sometimes if I wouldn't have gotten those beatings, I might not have turned out to be the nice person I am. It taught me to be polite and kind to the people around me.

If I were going to give advice to other kids, I'd say, "Watch the different signs and watch the way people do things. Just be aware of your surroundings. The person who might hurt you sexually can be the person you least suspect."

The thought of talking openly with an adult about sexual abuse might make you feel uncomfortable. But as you learned from Phillip, talking is a great way to learn what sexual abuse is. Talking is a great way to learn what sexual abuse is and what to do if you're approached. It's also a great way to learn how to stay safe.

Another important thing you can do to stay safe is listen to the little voice inside you. You know the one that says, "Something isn't right," or "This doesn't feel good," or "I don't feel safe." Anytime you hear that voice or get that funny feeling inside your tummy, something probably isn't right and you should tell a trusting adult right away.

Remember: Talking is a great way to learn what sexual

abuse is and what to do if you're approached. It's also a great way to learn how to stay safe. It's also the best thing to do if something doesn't feel right.

Chapter 9

It's Not Your Fault

Christopher's Story

My name is Christopher. One day this guy, Jason, moved next door to us. I was outside cutting the grass – my stepfather made me – when Jason came over and said hello. He invited me to his house to see this old sports car that he just bought and was going to fix up. It was the coolest thing I'd ever seen. Inside, his garage was filled with posters from all these famous race car drivers, and a lot of the posters had real autographs.

Jason asked if I'd like to help him work on his car. I couldn't believe it. Since my mom and dad divorced, I didn't really have anyone to do that kind of stuff with. My mom remarried, but my new stepfather and I didn't get along. He wanted me to do everything his way. And sometimes I didn't think there was anything wrong with the way I used to do it. After all, he wasn't my dad or anything. But my mom would say, just do it his way. I did what he wanted, but I didn't like it and I stayed away from him as much as I could.

But Jason wasn't like my stepfather, he was cool. He treated me like a real man, hanging out, working on his car, and sometimes he'd even let me have a cigarette. One time he showed me some adult Internet sites. He said it was okay because I was mature for my age, and it was normal for boys to be interested in sex.

After we'd been hanging out a few weeks, we finished up doing some stuff around his house, and he invited me to stay for pizza and watch a pay-per-view fight on television. We put our feet on the coffee table – that's something I'd never be allowed to do at home. I liked being with Jason. He always made me feel like I was smart and grown-up, not like I was just a kid who didn't do anything right.

When the pizza came, I couldn't believe it. He ordered me a large one of my own. Then he got up, went to the refrigerator and took out two beers. I thought they were for him, but he handed one to me. A beer for me, a high school kid? My stepfather would never do that.

In between rounds, Jason moved from his chair to the other end of the couch, opposite me. At first we laughed and ate nachos and made fun of the commercials and stuff. But then when I looked over, he was touching himself, right in front of me. I couldn't believe it. I didn't look and tried to pretend like it wasn't really happening, but it was. I kept eating my pizza and drinking, like it wasn't really happening.

After a few minutes I started getting nervous and warm all over, like I needed to get out of there. But I didn't know what to do. I couldn't just get up. So I sat there and watched the fight and acted like it never happened.

When I left that night I didn't go back for a few weeks. I felt mixed-up about it all. I mean, he had a girlfriend and stuff. She was really pretty. So, I kept wondering why he did it, and I wondered if he thought I wanted him to do it.

The next time I saw him, he asked me why I hadn't been coming over. He said he really liked me, and he said he wanted to show me all the progress he made on his car. I told him I was busy, and I'd been spending a lot of time at school practicing for the basketball team. I didn't have a hoop at home.

The very next day when I got home from school, Jason had a basketball hoop installed in his driveway. I couldn't believe it. When I asked my mom for a hoop, she said I had to ask my stepfather. I wasn't about to ask him, so I said forget it. He wouldn't have said yes anyway, so why bother. But Jason put one up for me. I kept thinking that maybe he was trying to apologize for what he did.

I started spending time with him again. He helped me with my skill shots and defensive moves, and I made the team. I was so excited that I went straight from school to tell him. We had a great night, shooting hoops, watching football, drinking beer. But then, he did it again, he moved to the sofa. This time, though, instead of touching himself, he reached over and touched me. I didn't know what to do. I just sat there and let him do it.

Then, when he was done, he told me if I ever told anyone, he would spread the word that I was gay. He said he'd tell everyone I asked him to do it to me. I didn't want anyone to find out. I'm not gay. I like girls, not guys, and I didn't want him to touch me. It's just that I liked hanging out with him. He made me feel, I don't know, special – grown-up – and besides, I didn't know what to do.

For the rest of the school year, I tried to stay away from Jason, but he'd call and ask my mom if I could go out for a pizza or shoot some hoops or something. My mom thought he was a really nice guy. She kept asking me why I didn't want to see him anymore. She wanted to know if something happened, but I couldn't tell her. I wanted to, but I just couldn't. So, when I'd say no, when I'd tell him I was busy or whatever, she'd tell me that I should play basketball with him since he bought that hoop just for me. So I did it, because I didn't want her to be mad at me, and I didn't want to tell her what happened. I didn't want her to know. I didn't want anyone to know. But most of all, I really didn't want my stepfather to know.

Then one day, in the middle of the summer, when I got home from the neighborhood pool, Jason was at my house asking my mom if he could take me to the drive-in. She thought that was so nice and said yes, as long as he took my little brother and sister. She had a bingo party to go to, and I was supposed to baby-sit for my little brother and sister. To tell you the truth, I was glad they were going along, I really wanted to see the movie, and I didn't think he'd do anything in front of them.

When we got to the drive-in, Jason made my brother and sister sit outside in the grass and watch the movie while he and I were inside the car. I thought it was because we were going to have a beer or a cigarette or something. But that's when he did it to me again. All I could think about was whether or not my little brother and sister could see inside the windows, whether or not they knew what was going on, and if they would tell anyone. I didn't care what he did to me as much as what people would think if they found out, so I didn't fight too much or yell or anything. I just let him do it, and I didn't tell anyone.

When we got home, I went right to my room, but my little brother and sister were all bit up from the bugs in the grass, and my mom wanted to know what was going on. They told her he made them sit outside and he was in the car with me. Then they told her that he pushed me down, they could see him on top of me in the front seat. My mom called me downstairs after she got them tucked into bed and asked me what happened.

It was awful having to tell her, worse than I thought. And my stepfather stood there, shaking his head. I knew he was thinking it was my fault, even though he didn't say it. He probably thought I was this weakling who couldn't take care of myself. I should have been able to stop him. I should have pushed him off me, or fought, or done something. But I didn't. I thought, if I'm too stupid or weak to protect myself, then it's my own fault.

My mom called the police, and I had to tell them the story. Then I had to tell the District Attorney, and then I had to tell the doctor at the hospital. It was the worst thing I'd ever gone through. I was so humiliated, and all the while my stepfather just kept shaking his head, like he was saying, "This is your own fault." I know that's what he was thinking. But it's not true. I just didn't know what to do. My little brother and sister were right outside the car.

Later, my mom told me that the police said he did the same thing to a few other kids in the neighborhood where he used to live. But none of that mattered to me. I couldn't stand thinking about what he did or knowing that so many people knew. I hated myself. I wanted to die. I didn't want to leave my room, or go to school, or talk to my friends or my family. I started fighting with my stepfather all the time. I didn't care what he wanted me to do, cut the grass or take out the trash, I just wasn't going to do it. We'd end up in this big fight, with my little brother and sister crying and calling for my mom. And my mom would be crying and yelling that we needed to get along and saying she just couldn't take all this. But I didn't care. I wanted him to hit me, or beat me, or kill me. I didn't care. I didn't want to live with him or anyone else.

When school started the following year, I didn't join the basketball team. I don't know, I just felt different, queer, weird. I didn't want to shower in front of the other guys; I didn't want them to know. I don't know, I was afraid that somehow they'd know my secret.

I couldn't get it out of my head, what he did to me, or the feeling that everyone knew. I hated myself for being a weakling. I wanted to die. That's when I did it. I went into the bathroom and swallowed all the pills in the medicine cabinet. I don't even know what they were for, or what would happen if I lived. I didn't care.

My mom found me. She said I was passed out and that an ambulance took me to the hospital. They pumped my stomach, and I had to stay in the hospital for a while.

I guess I'm doing a little better now, but I'll never forget what happened. Even though my counselor says it wasn't my fault, I can't help thinking it was. I should have known better, or been able to stop him or something.

I'm glad my mom was there for me. Sometimes she even went to counseling with me. I don't think I could have made it without her. My stepfather has been really trying, too. He's even taken me to some ball games and spent time with me. I guess he's okay. I don't know. I'm not sure what to think about myself or anyone any more.

My mom wants me to try out for the basketball team again next year. I'll be a senior, and she says it's really important that I do as much as I can since it's my last year. I'm not sure if I want to, but I told her I'd think about it. Right now, it's all I can do to just get up and get through the day. Sometimes it's really hard; sometimes I guess it's okay. My counselor keeps telling me that it wasn't my fault, and I shouldn't blame myself. But I still do. I mean I'm trying to believe my counselor and listen because he really knows what it's like. But, it's hard. He says this will take time, a long time. I just wish it would go away.

Here's my advice for kids, "If anyone does anything like this to you, don't wait until it's too late. Even if they make you feel grown-up, or let you do things you're not allowed to do, tell an adult right away."

✳✳✳

As Christopher learned, sexual abusers are so good at what they do that you might not even realize what's happening. Often they start out slowly, spending time with you, building a friendship. They will encourage you to spend time alone with them. And they will tell you things to make you feel good about yourself, like how handsome you are, how special you are, or what a terrific kid you are.

To help the relationship get stronger, and to encourage you to trust them, abusers will offer to take you special places, like camping, the movies or the mall. They may even buy you gifts like clothes, CDs or video games – things you said you liked and may have even asked for.

As your relationship with the abuser grows, sometimes he or she will allow you to do things you're not allowed to do at home or at school, like smoke cigarettes, drink beer, watch certain programs on television, or visit adult Internet sites. An abuser will do whatever he or she can to make you feel comfortable and convince you that the two of you have a special relationship no one else shares.

When the abuser feels confident in your trust, he or she will slowly introduce you to sexual activity that progresses over time. At first, you might not be sure what is happening. The abuser might rub up against you or touch you over your clothes while tickling, wrestling, or playing in some way. The abuser might accidentally walk in on you when you're in the bathroom, or let you see him or her doing something sexual, or watching pornography.

As time progresses, the sexual activities will happen more often, and eventually you'll realize that you and the abuser have a secret relationship, not a good secret relationship but a scary secret relationship. No matter how long it lasts, or what the abuser did to trick you into doing the secret sexual activities, it's not your fault.

Remember: Sexual abusers are so good at what they do that you might not even realize what's happening. But any time you are tricked or forced into sexual activity with someone, it's never your fault and you should tell someone right away!

Chapter 10

Lynn's Story

My name is Lynn. I'm a 16-year-old high school junior. Right now I'm working on getting my driver's license, but my mom still gets really nervous when I drive. When I'm not driving or playing with the new puppies my dog just had, I love to take photographs, and I love little kids. My high school has a nursery school and a kindergarten class in the building, and I spend as much time there as I can, helping the kids, teachers and even the parents.

I think I like to be with little kids and make things better for them because my life growing up wasn't all that great. I lived with my mom, younger brother and dad. My dad was like a ticking time bomb. He had a bad temper. The slightest little thing would set him off and he'd freak out on everybody. It was uncomfortable because I never knew when it was going to happen or what would make it happen. When he'd freak out on my mom, I always stuck up for her. One time it was really bad. He had her by the arm and started twisting it. He said he was going to break her arm, so I started punching him, kicking him and trying to protect her. It felt good that I was sticking up for my mom, but I was scared to death.

The secret relationship with my dad started out slow. Anytime my mom wasn't home, my dad would just start giving me lots of hugs and kisses, and he'd start touching me. Then he'd tell me not to say anything or I'd go to jail and, of course, since I was only seven, I believed him. It was really scary for me. When I got older he just kept doing more, but I didn't believe that I'd go to jail anymore. That's when he started to threaten me, saying he was going to kill me if I told. He also used to tell me that if I told, he'd go to jail, but when he got out he'd come after me. I believed him. So I just stayed quiet, and it went on for eight years.

It happened everywhere. It happened all the time. It seemed like there wasn't anywhere for me to go. I didn't have a safe place. He did it to me in my room, in the living room, in the kitchen. One time my dad, my brother and I went to a park. We were supposed to go walking on some trails. My dad told us that we'd each take our own trail, but as soon as my brother started down his path, my dad took me with him. We didn't get very far.

Another time my whole family went camping – my grandparents, aunt and uncle, mom, little brother, dad and me. My mom told me that I had to stay with my dad because everyone else was going shopping for my birthday. I was going to be ten that year. I cried and begged her to let me go along. I said I'd go into a different store or I'd wait outside.

But she said no. She said I had to stay with my dad. So they all went shopping and left me there with him. And when they got home I had to act like nothing happened.

It happened at different places along the way, like when he'd pick me up from a friend's house. I hated it when he'd pick me up. He'd always take a detour home. One time it happened on the way home from my cousin's birthday party. Of course he couldn't be the one to stay home with my sick little brother; he had to be the one to pick me up. On the way home, it happened right down the road from my cousin's house.

I always felt safe at my grandparents' house and I loved to be with them. Every year I went on vacation with them. But when I'd get back, the abuse was always twice as much as before. Because I was gone, because I wasn't there when he wanted to do something, I'd be punished. And that's when he would hurt me.

As time went on, things with my dad got worse. It happened more often, and he got more violent. One time, I was bleeding so much that I thought I was going to die. But he just said, "Oh, you're all right." But I didn't feel all right. I was scared.

No matter what he did to me, no matter how much he hurt me, afterwards, he'd always apologize and say, "You know I love you, right?" Then he'd say, "You love me, too, right?" And he'd make me answer him. So I'd say "right," but I crossed my fingers because I didn't want to lie even though I didn't mean it.

And to make things worse, my dad always told me he wanted to try it with one of my friends. So I kept my friends away from him. I only had one friend over to my house the whole time he was doing it to me, and I kept my eye on her every minute. I never let her out of my sight. I just couldn't take a chance that he might do something to her.

The whole time my dad was abusing me, I felt horrible – horrible and scared – and just, yuck. It changed the way I saw myself. I was different than I used to be. I can't really explain it, but I felt like I was different than all the other kids. I felt like I was the only kid this had ever happened to and, because of it, I felt like I wasn't as good as the other kids. I felt like I had this awful secret, and I was terrified that if my friends found out they wouldn't like me.

I also had trouble going to sleep because he would come into my room at night. I'd force myself to stay awake until I just couldn't stay awake anymore. I was always exhausted. I couldn't concentrate in school, and my grades dropped. All I could think about was, "What am I going to do, where am I going to go, so I don't have to go home." When my dad did it to me, he used to say that it was a punishment. He said I deserved it because I had done something wrong. I knew my bad grades just gave him more reason to punish me – more reason to keep abusing me.

I thought a lot about running away, but I just couldn't leave my mom and my brother with him. I didn't know what he'd do to them if I ran away. I felt like I had to protect them. I felt that if I stayed and went along with what he wanted, it would be better for them.

I felt all alone and out of control, and I had all this anger. But I didn't do anything outwardly. I just held it all inside. I used to think about killing myself and cutting myself, but I just couldn't do it. Instead I turned to food for comfort.

I clung to my teddy bear, too. He was like my best friend, a friend my dad couldn't hurt, a friend that no matter what my dad did, I could always have close to me. And I don't know how, but I think having my teddy bear there made a difference for me. He kept me sane.

I also wrote in a journal, but I did it more hoping my mom would find it. I kept it where I thought she might see it. I wanted her to find my journal in case something happened to me. That way she would know he did it, and she wouldn't stay with him anymore.

The other thing I did was cause fights with my dad. My mom always said that he'd be "out of there" if he ever hit me, so I'd try to make him angry. I'd throw fits and just say things to get him angry, like the one time – it was the stupidest thing – when the dishes needed to be washed. My mom told me to do the dishes and I said, "No. Why don't you make dad do them? He wouldn't do them if his life depended on it." That was when the time bomb blew up. He came after me. I was sitting in a chair, and he threw it backwards. Then he grabbed me by the hair and just started punching me. I was thinking "yes, yes" he's finally going to get kicked out, but that never happened. That's when I felt like it was never going to end.

Then, one day I was at my aunt's house. It was right before Halloween. She and I were sitting in the basement talking. I don't even know how we got on the subject, but she started telling me about one of her boyfriends. She told me how he was always trying to do sexual stuff to her that she didn't want him to do. My aunt said she was hoping that would never happen to me – that I would never be raped or anything. When my aunt said that, I just started crying – she couldn't believe it. She started freaking out, and we both cried for an hour.

The next day she took me to the police station, and she told our friend, the chief of police, what was going on. He wanted me to give him a statement, and I told him everything. That was Sunday night. On Monday, I went to school, and when I came home, my mom and my aunt were home from work early, and they were crying.

I was too scared to say anything because I didn't know what my aunt was thinking, and I didn't know what my mom was going to do. So I just acted like I didn't know what was going on. They told me that the police went to my dad's work that day and arrested him.

I didn't think it would happen so fast, but it felt really good to know he was arrested. It felt even better to know my mom and aunt were so mad at my dad, and that they believed me. I found out later that, after my dad was arrested, he called his mom and asked her to help him get out, but she was really mad at him, too. She said he did a terrible thing and that he deserved to be in jail. I was so glad she didn't try to help him get out.

When I got into counseling, it really helped. Jaime, my counselor, keeps me sane. In the beginning, it was hard for me to talk to someone I didn't really know, but after a little time, I was able to open up and tell her what happened and how I was feeling.

Counseling is a process; sometimes I feel like I go three

steps forward and one back, but I know I'm getting better. Jaime keeps telling me I'm so much better now than I was in the beginning. She says I'm able to talk more about what happened. She says I know my emotions better now and I can let them out.

I think the best part about getting counseling was learning that it wasn't my fault and that I didn't deserve or ask to be abused. My dad used to always tell me that the reason he did it to me was because I had done something wrong – it was my punishment. I really thought I deserved it. But Jaime helped me know that wasn't true. She showed me that kids never deserve to be abused; kids never ask for it – no matter what they do.

I think my experiences have made me stronger and more focused. I think they have also made me more mature than a lot of the kids I go to school with. But, the best part of it all is that, because of what happened, I can trust my mom more than I ever thought I could. I can tell her things I never thought I could.

If I could give advice to kids I'd tell them, "If this is happening to you, find someone you can trust and tell that person immediately. It doesn't matter if you're being threatened, find someone and tell them immediately! What's happening to you isn't your fault. You don't deserve to be sexually abused, no matter what your abuser says to you."

If I could give advice to adults, I'd say, "Ask your kids if they're all right. Your kids might not be okay, and they probably don't know how to tell you. Look for signs, changes – your kids might be doing things hoping you'll notice that something is wrong."

✳✳✳

As Lynn learned, sexual abusers do a lot of things to get kids involved in sexual activities. They also do as much as they can to keep kids quiet and keep the sexual activities ongoing. When Lynn's dad abused her, he told her she was being punished. When he wanted to be sure she wouldn't tell anyone, he threatened her. Some abusers will also threaten to hurt someone close to you, someone you love, or someone you care about.

They might also tell you that no one will believe you. They might say you asked for it, or you deserved it. They might tell you that if you tell someone, you will be blamed and punished for what happened. They might say they are the only ones who love you. They might say that if you tell, they will stop loving you, stop taking you special places, and stop buying you nice things.

These are all threatening and silencing tactics that abusers use to keep kids quiet and keep sexual relationships ongoing. But remember, if someone has tricked or forced you into any type of sexual activity, it's never your fault. Never!

Remember: A sexual abuser will work very hard to get you involved in a secret sexual relationship. He or she will work just as hard to keep you involved and often will frighten, threaten, or trick you to keep you quiet. But no matter what an abuser says, you should tell a trusting adult right away.

Chapter 11

You're Not Alone

John's Story

I was little when it started, four or five years old. My parents both worked, and this man named Wayne would come by and play with me. He took me to a place that, to me, felt like we were out in the country. Since I lived in the city, when I went for a long drive that ended up where there were few houses or people and mostly trees, to me it felt like being in the country. That's where he started touching me.

Our relationship grew over time. We spent a lot of time together. I liked Wayne and I trusted him. I don't really know why I kept going along with him, but I liked the way he made me feel special. My parents were gone all the time, and when they were home, they didn't have the time or energy to spend with me, my brother or sister. They were always busy making dinner, doing laundry or relaxing. So, I liked it when this older guy paid attention to me and spent time with me.

After he started touching me, he told me it was our special

secret and said I couldn't tell anyone about it. He also let me do things I wasn't allowed to do, like taste beer and smoke cigarettes. And he'd always buy me things and give me money. At the time, I thought he just liked me, but now I'm pretty sure he did it to keep me quiet.

Wayne really didn't need to worry about me telling anyone, because my dad was a disciplinarian and I knew what we were doing – our secret relationship – was bad. I was afraid that if I told my parents, they'd be mad at me, maybe even blame and punish me. I was so afraid that I didn't say anything, and our relationship just continued and continued.

One day a policeman came to our house and said he was investigating Wayne. He said Wayne had touched a lot of the kids in our neighborhood and wanted to know if he touched me, too. I said no. I think I protected him because I still liked him. Even though I didn't really like what he was doing to me, I liked the attention, and I liked the things he bought me and the things he let me do.

Before it all started, I was a happy kid. I think I was a regular kid. But after it started, I changed. I became the class clown because I didn't want anyone to see what was really going on. I wanted everyone to think I had it all together. I wanted everyone to think I was in control.

But I wasn't. My grades fell and, after a little while, I was put in special classes for kids with learning problems. In those classes, they didn't really teach me anything, so I just went along from year to year and never learned anything. Then when I was a junior in high school, we had to take a test and, all of a sudden, everyone said I shouldn't have been put in the special classes. Right away they pulled me out and put me in the regular classes with the kids who had been learning all along. The first assignment I got was to do a book report. I had never done a book report before. I hadn't even read a book before. I was totally lost.

After that I didn't care anymore. That's when I got into drugs, heavy. I tried every drug that was out there, and when I wasn't doing drugs, I was drinking. I was either drunk or high all the time.

I always had sexual urges, too. From the time I was younger I had a lot of them, all the time. I had them so much; it was hard for me to handle them. I tried to hide them. I tried to control myself, but I couldn't. I'd have to go sneaking off to the bathroom two or three times a day, every day.

I was also mixed-up about my own sexuality. I felt confused all the time. I had a steady girlfriend who really cared about me. One day we had a fight, and right away I started thinking about being with guys instead of girls. I even experimented behind her back. That made me feel really bad, guilty and dirty, especially because I knew she really liked me.

Sometimes I used to do things to hurt myself, like burn myself, in private places. I don't know if I was mad because my sexual urges came so often or because I felt confused about wanting to be with guys or girls. Maybe I did it because I just didn't like myself or what happened to me. Now I know I have all these urges because of my abuse.

One of the things that helped me get through everything was drawing and painting. I love making psychedelic drawings with bright colors. I started doing it right after the police came and took Wayne away. I did it when I was high, I did it when I was sad, I did it when I felt confused. And I still do it now, sometimes because I just need to express myself, sometimes because I need to get the feelings out – separate from me. Then, when I'm done, I can put the drawings and paintings and my feelings away if I want to. That always helps.

I got into a counseling group not too long ago. My first few times, everyone was talking about what happened to them, and they were all helping and supporting each other. They were really open about what they had been through, and they made me feel comfortable right away. It really helped to know I wasn't the only one who had hard stuff to deal with.

I think counseling has also really helped me understand and deal with what I've been through. It's nice to know I'm not alone. If something about my abuse comes up that's hard for me to deal with alone, it's nice to know they're there, and they understand. I guess it's just nice to know there's someone I can talk to, someone who isn't going to judge me, especially since I still don't always feel very good about myself.

I got sober, stopped using drugs and managed to graduate from high school. But I don't have any plans for my future. I'm just trying to get through this abuse stuff and have a normal life and a normal relationship with my girlfriend. But, maybe someday I'll go to college and get more education. I'm just not sure.

There was a time when I think my mom really knew what was going on. She didn't say anything or do anything, but I still think she suspected. But she never came out and asked me. She never asked if I was all right. She never asked what Wayne and I did or where we went when we were together. And she never made me feel like it would be okay to talk about it, so I just stayed quiet.

Recently my sister told me that Wayne took advantage of her, too. That really made me feel bad, even worse than I felt about what happened to me. I wondered if I had said something, or if my mom had asked, maybe she wouldn't have been hurt. I also wondered if Wayne did the same thing to my brother, too. I hope all the other kids he touched don't have as hard of a time with it as I do. Even though I know I'm getting better, it's been really hard.

If I were going to give advice, I think I'd really want to talk to parents more than kids. Parents need to talk to their kids, and they need to make it okay for kids to tell them things without worrying about being punished or blamed.

As far as advice for kids, I think I'd say, "You might think you're the only one, like I did. I wasn't the only one, and the person abusing you is probably abusing other kids, too, so tell someone. I know it's hard, and if it's too hard for you to tell your parents, like it was for me, maybe you can find someone else to tell."

✳ ✳ ✳

As John learned, abusers work very hard to make you feel special. They pay attention to you when other adults are too busy. They might buy you things, take you places or let you do things you're not allowed to do. Sometimes they will even tell you you're pretty or handsome, or say they love you. Often they will make you think you're the only one. They might even tell you that, as long as you stay quiet, they won't do it to other kids. Usually sexual abusers don't limit themselves to just one child, or do it just one time. Often they victimize many children. Sometimes hundreds of kids are victimized by just one person.

If you are being sexually abused, chances are, the person abusing you is abusing other kids, too. Even if you feel like you're the only one, even if they tell you you're the only one, you're probably not.

Remember: You're not alone. If you're being victimized, the person abusing you will probably trick or force other kids into sexual activity, too. Get safe and stay safe. Tell a trusting adult today!

Chapter 12

Why Do I Feel the Way I Do?

Susan's Story

Growing up, I lived in an average neighborhood with my mom, sister, older brother and dad. For as long as I can remember, I was always a shy, overweight kid. I didn't play with many kids, and sometimes I got picked on at school. But the first time I remember anything really bad happening to me was when a group of fifth grade boys pulled me into the bushes and lifted my shirt. I told the teacher, but she said they were just "boys being boys." That made me feel like what they did to me wasn't that bad, or maybe I deserved it. That was the starting point for me. I became a target; the boys would always pick on me, follow me home and call me names. I felt powerless, because even when I told a teacher about it, no one helped me.

Shortly after that, I spent the night at a girlfriend's house. My friend was asleep when her mother's boyfriend came into the bedroom. He lay behind me and began rubbing himself against me, rubbing his hands on me. I didn't like it. It didn't feel good. I was inside a sleeping bag but that didn't stop him. He still kept rubbing his hands on me. It seemed like it was never going to stop. Then her mother walked into the room and told him to leave me alone. Even though she saw what he was doing, she didn't do anything about it.

I left so quickly the next morning, I forgot my glasses. My mom was really angry with me for leaving them, and she took me back to get them. I told her I didn't like him and I didn't want to go in. She yelled at me, and made me go inside. The boyfriend was sitting on the chair with my glasses in his hand. He made me climb onto his lap and he pulled me into his crotch and rubbed me up against him.

I grabbed my glasses and ran back to the car. My mom asked me what was wrong, but when I told her what he did, she made excuses. She said he was probably just rubbing my back. I felt like my mom didn't understand what I was trying to say. I felt like she didn't want to hear me. She didn't do anything to protect me, either.

In the sixth grade, one of my brother's friends took my clothes off and took pictures of me. My brother would never have let him do that, but he wasn't there. His friend was one of the boys who harassed me the year before. Now he was bigger and still bothering me. But this time he was in my house taking pictures of me. I felt like I wasn't safe anywhere.

I felt like all the older boys knew what those boys were doing to me. I felt so ashamed. They called me "Susie the slut," like I wanted it, but I didn't. I was afraid of them, and I didn't know how to fight back. I felt like no one would help me, and I didn't know how to stop them. I don't know why, maybe because I didn't fight back, I felt responsible, like I asked for it, like it was my fault.

When I started dating, I became more of a target. Ron was my first serious boyfriend and my first sexual experience. I was 16, and it was the end of my freshman year. The relationship was never good.

He'd be mean to me one minute and nice the next. I guess I thought some girls deserved it when boys were mean or hurtful to them. Whenever he was mean I thought it was my fault, and I'd cry and beg him to forgive me.

One day we were in the middle of having sex, and I started thinking about another boy – a boy I felt safe with, a boy who was nice to me, one I wished I could be with. I said this other kid's name instead of Ron's. Ron didn't even hesitate; right then, he pulled back and punched me in the face. Then he finished having sex with me. I felt like it was my fault. I stayed with Ron after that and he was rougher and hurt me more. I felt like I gave him the signal that he could treat me that way. I felt like I deserved it.

That's when things got even worse for me. I couldn't sleep at all. I was frightened to change in front of other girls. I didn't want to be in coed gym glasses. I started taking diet pills and became bulimic. It was the only sense of control I had.

My mom started asking me, "What's going on with you? What's wrong with you?" I wanted to tell her, but I didn't know how, so I wrote her a letter. But she just dismissed it. That was really hard for me. It was even harder that my older brother didn't do anything about it either. I expected him to get mad and want to protect me, but when he didn't, that really hurt.

After that I spent a lot of time in the nurse's office. I think the nurse knew something was wrong, but she didn't push me to tell her. She was the first person who ever cried for me. That was very powerful and made me feel like someone cared. But when I told her what was going on with Ron, she said there's nothing I could do except break up with him.

I broke up with Ron, and I got another boyfriend, but that relationship wasn't any better. If I didn't want to have sex, he'd force me. But when he did that to me, I didn't say anything – I just let him get away with it. I thought that's what it was like for everyone. He cheated on me. I knew it but I didn't do anything about it. Then he started hitting me, hurting me sexually and calling me names. I put up with that, too. I had learned to accept all kinds of cruelty.

One time we were in the car – I was driving. He started talking about another girl that he was intimate with. I got mad. I said, "If sex is all you want, I'll give it to you right now." I started stripping in the car. I was really mad. It was my way of standing up for myself – it was the first time I ever yelled back. He punched me, and we almost crashed, but he didn't care. He kept hitting me, and I couldn't swing back because I was trying to control the car. When he was finished, I said it was over, but I didn't do anything about it. My father used to hit us like that, so I just accepted it.

After that, I stopped taking care of myself. I didn't shower. I didn't go to the bathroom. I'd hold it until it hurt. By then, the bulimia was getting pretty bad and I felt like a zombie. I started blacking out in school. One time, they had to take me out of school in a wheelchair. But no one asked if I was okay or what was going on. I think the teachers were aware, but no one approached me or asked what was wrong. It was just another signal that you don't tell, you don't say anything. People just don't want to know. You're supposed to keep it to yourself.

I was so depressed and angry at the world, so helpless and hopeless that things wouldn't get any better – that I tried to kill myself. After a stay in the hospital, I started journaling and reading and trying to figure out what happened and how I managed to survive all this. Then it came to me – if I survived this, I can survive anything.

I knew I had to leave to change things, and I decided when I went to college, I'd go away. I also knew that I had to get myself together before I could have a healthy relationship. So I promised myself to wait for three years before getting into another relationship. That's when things became clearer.

It's funny because, even though I felt totally alone, I had a friend the whole time I was going through all this stuff. She was on the fringes of my life, but she was always there. She would tell me to find the positive in what happens. For a long time, I thought that wasn't true. But when I took some time to myself, I realized that although all these things happened, there were people out there who didn't treat others badly. I also began to see myself differently – better. The better I saw myself and the better I treated myself, the better the people around me saw me and treated me.

I really want to help children and protect them from what I went through. I really want to be there if kids need

111

someone to talk to.

If I could give advice to kids I'd say, "If you can survive abuse, you can survive anything." I'd also say, "Be the kind of person you want to be around. Set standards and boundaries. Respect yourself, and make others respect you, too."

✷ ✷ ✷

As you can see from Susan's story, she had many negative reactions to her abuse. She had difficulty concentrating in school, which led to failing grades. She cut herself and developed eating disorders. When Susan started to date, she allowed herself to continue to be hurt.

If someone has sexually abused you, you might have many different feelings and reactions, and your feelings might change from one day to the next. That's normal. It's your way of dealing with what has happened to you.

You might have trouble sleeping, or wake up in the middle of the night with terrible nightmares. You might have headaches or stomachaches. You might find yourself suddenly afraid of certain people or places, or you might not want to leave someone, like your mother, who makes you feel safe.

You might have trouble concentrating in school, your grades might begin to fall, or you might find that things you used to do easily have become difficult. Additionally, you might find yourself doing things like wetting the bed, sucking your thumb, talking like a baby or doing other child-like (regressive) behaviors that you don't understand.

Another reaction to sexual abuse is depression. Depression is a feeling of deep sadness that lasts a long time. When you're depressed you might lose interest in the things you used to love, like going to the mall, or playing ball with your buddies. Or, you might find yourself pulling away from people all together, staying in your room, not taking phone calls, and not wanting to socialize with your friends.

You might also feel responsible for what has happened; thinking you should have been smart enough or strong enough to stop it. You might feel guilty for letting it happen in the first place, thinking that something you did caused it. Or, you might feel dirty because you were touched in private places. That might make you want to wash all the time, or hide yourself under layers of clothing.

Sometimes kids who are sexually abused feel "damaged." You might be afraid that if your secret is discovered, you won't be loved or accepted. You might try extra hard to fit in, sometimes going along with the crowd, even when they do things you don't want to do, even when they do things you know are wrong.

Anger is another normal reaction to being abused and feeling out of control within your life. Sometimes kids hurt other kids to release the bad feelings they have inside. Some kids turn anger inside and hurt themselves by cutting or burning.

You might also have confused feelings about sex. You might have urges to repeat the activities that have been done to you. You might also find yourself engaging in risky sexual activities.

Although we've talked about many reactions to abuse, your reaction might be different. That's okay. No matter how you're reacting, it's important to remember it's normal – it's your way of surviving what you've been through. But it's also important to remember that your reactions can be hurtful to you and others. However, with the help of trusting adults, you can heal from your abuse, stop the destructive behavior and live a full and happy life.

Remember: Reacting to sexual abuse is normal. But reacting in ways that are destructive can be hurtful to you. Tell someone what's going on and get help!

Chapter 13

What if They Don't Believe Me?

Tracy's Story

I moved to Florida with my grandparents right before I turned 16. The church that we went to was right down our street. I could see it from my grandma's house. My pastor's son, Mike, was 21, and I hung out with him all the time. He used to go to my high school, and he knew a lot of kids there. He hung out at the church, too. He was our youth leader and he was there all the time. I liked him, and I'd flirt with him. He kissed me once, and I kissed him back. I was happy.

One day I went to our high school soccer game, and Mike was there. When it was over, he said he'd take me home. I called my grandma, and she was fine with it because he was the pastor's son. Who's not going to trust him? When he took me home, he kissed me, and I kissed him back. We had done that before. But this time, he kept going. I told him to stop, and he didn't. It went on. I told him to stop again, but he was bigger than me. Mike used to wrestle in high school, so I was no match for his strength. He completely took advantage of me. I suppose it was a date rape.

When I got home, I went straight to the shower and scrubbed and scrubbed. I think I was trying to make it go away, but I couldn't. I was so upset. I wanted to tell my grandma, but I couldn't. I didn't know how. I watched a movie once with my grandparents, and when a girl was raped, my grandfather said it was all her fault. He said she asked for it. My grandma agreed. So I didn't know how to tell them. I think, deep inside, I was afraid they'd say the same thing about me. I think I was afraid they'd say it was my fault.

That night I called my friend. Since I had just moved, I didn't have a lot of friends, but I knew my best friend would understand, because it had just happened to her, too. The guy she was dating did it to her. We talked about what happened, and I was glad I had someone to talk to.

Before I was raped, I was really a people person. I was always willing to talk to people if they needed help or someone to listen to their problems. But after I was raped, I felt like I didn't help or listen to people as much as I used to. I guess I felt that nobody listened to me. And I thought, how am I ever going to listen to other people's problems when they can't listen to mine?

Afterwards, I know my attitude changed, and my clothes definitely changed, too. I couldn't hide that, and I know my grandma noticed. I used to wear short shorts and stuff, but after it happened, I always wore baggy T-shirts and blue jeans, no matter how hot it was. Even in my own pool, I wore a T-shirt over my bathing suit. It was an open pool and, when

I was out there, I'd think about how the pastor's son was in the church right down the road. I just didn't feel safe, I guess. But at school, I didn't let myself think about what he did. Instead of thinking about it, I purely focused on my activities, the Flag Corp and the singing group that I belonged to.

A few days after it happened, my grandmother sat me down and asked me what was going on, what happened, why I was dressing and acting differently. When I told her about the night my pastor's son brought me home, I said, "He raped me, grandma." She told me I probably asked for it. I know she was talking about how I dressed. My grandma didn't like the way I dressed, so she assumed I asked for it. She assumed it was my fault that he raped me. I wasn't a virgin. I had a steady boyfriend before that and she knew it. She didn't like that, either.

I kept insisting that Mike did it, and I didn't ask for it, and she said, "Right, sure. He's the pastor's son." It was like she was defending him, trying to tell me that he was brought up not to do stuff like that. It was like she was trying to convince me it was my fault. I was so mad.

After my grandma and I were done talking, I went to my room and starting scribbling in a journal. I drew these hard, thick black lines all over the page. I couldn't believe that she honestly didn't believe me. She took care of me, she loved me, but she didn't believe me. I didn't tell anyone else after that, just my friend. I didn't want to take a chance that anyone else would blame me.

About a month later, another youth leader must have noticed my changes, and that I was staying far away from

Mike. After a church activity, the youth leader took me home, and we stopped to pick up a pizza. He asked me what happened, but before I could even answer or open my mouth, he asked, "Did Mike rape you?" I was shocked. I didn't answer him, but I nodded and I kept wondering how he knew. I was wondering if, maybe, Mike did it to other girls in the group, too. I don't know why no one ever did anything about it. No charges were brought against him or anything. But I was glad because I didn't want to deal with "He's the pastor's son" and, "You wear skimpy clothes" and, "You're not even a virgin," and have people saying it was my fault.

My experience really changed me. I'm lucky that I had a lot of activities at school to focus on. I didn't let myself think about what happened, I just made myself think about the stuff I had to do, like my flag routines. But I got really aggressive after that – aggressive about protecting myself, like when a guy came up to me and I didn't want to talk to him. Instead of just walking away or ignoring him, I'd get in his face and tell him to leave me alone.

I was aggressive with the boys I wanted to be with, too. I had another relationship right after Mike abused me. I got close to John, right away, and I thought he loved me as much as I loved him. Even though we were only together three months, I thought we were going to get married. But when I told him I was pregnant, he broke up with me. He said he didn't love me. He told me he loved someone else. He said he was going to marry her, not me.

That was probably it for me, because then I just let myself be with a lot of guys. I'm not sure why I did it. Maybe it's because I didn't have any self-esteem. Maybe it's because the two guys I really trusted hurt me. Maybe it's because I wanted to be in control. I don't know.

The following Christmas, my grandma, who was still close to the pastor and his wife, invited them over for dinner. Mike was supposed to come to dinner, too. I was so upset. I couldn't believe my grandma would do that to me. But when the pastor and his wife arrived, his wife told me that Mike wasn't coming because he had the flu. I said to her, "That's too bad," with this sarcasm in my voice. My grandmother just glared at me, and the pastor's wife gave me this strange look. But I didn't care, I was so glad he wasn't coming.

I think that's when my grandma realized that I had been telling the truth, because after that she was different. She starting saying things like, "No one deserves to be treated that way," and, "No one ever asks for it." I was glad to hear her say that, because I didn't ask for it, and I didn't do anything to deserve it. I only wish it wouldn't have taken her so long to figure it out.

It was so hard for me knowing that Mike was just a few doors away, and every time I looked at the church I knew he was right there. I had to be near him, and I had to see him. But it was even worse for me knowing that he got away with it. I only wish that all adults would listen to kids. No one is going to lie about being sexually abused. It doesn't matter what a girl dresses like, not at all; that doesn't mean she wants you to do anything to her. I can be at the beach in my bikini, or the library in my sweats, but either way, I'm not asking for it.

If I knew someone else went through what I did, they told

someone, and they weren't believed, I'd tell them, "Find someone who believes you. There's got to be someone you can tell who will believe you. Keep telling people until someone believes you."

✳✳✳

If you tell a trusting adult about abuse, like Tracy did, there's a possibility you won't be believed. It can be hard for grown-ups who love you to accept that someone has done something so terrible to hurt you. Like Tracy's grandmother, sometimes adults don't understand sexual abuse. They might blame you and say you asked for it. They might even say you deserved it, because of how you dressed or how you acted.

But that's not true! No matter how you dress or how you act, no one has the right to hurt you or take advantage of you in a sexual way. No one ever asks to be sexually abused. No one ever deserves to be sexually abused. If the first person you tell doesn't want to believe you, keep telling until you find someone who will.

Remember: No matter what anyone says, if you have been sexually abused, it's not your fault! If you tell someone and that person doesn't believe you, keep telling until you find someone who will believe you.

Chapter 14

Telling Is Hard, But It's Important

Hope's Story

My name is Hope. I was 12 when it happened to me. I went to my friend Gary's house. He was my age, and even though I was a girl and he was a guy, we used to hang out together and play basketball or other sports. One time, when I went to his house, this guy was there. He was a lot older than me and had just broken up with my older sister. He started telling me I was pretty and special; that really made me feel good. Then he started kissing me, and he got rough and pushed me down on the sofa. He held me down. I fought him and screamed, but he didn't stop and I wasn't strong enough to push him off.

I looked over at my friend Gary. He was sitting on the other side of the wrap-around sofa, pretending to be asleep. I know he was pretending because I was screaming and fighting, and there's no way he could have slept through that. But Gary didn't help me. Gary let this guy take complete advantage of me.

When I was able to get away, I ran out of Gary's house. For some reason, on my way home I pulled my shirt off. I don't know why. I think I was trying to peel my skin off my body and get away from the feeling I had when he touched me. At home, I went straight to the shower and tried to scrub myself clean.

I didn't talk to anyone about what happened to me at Gary's house. I masked my feelings, pretending everything was okay. But it wasn't. I felt terrible, guilty and all alone.

Even though I was really strong and independent, I needed someone to talk to. I wanted to tell my sister, but we never had a good relationship to start with. I was always more popular and thinner. I think that was hard for her. It put more distance between us.

When all this happened, especially since it was her ex-boyfriend, I was afraid she'd be angry with me. I was afraid she'd blame me or accuse me of trying to steal him. After all, I liked the way he was talking to me. He was a lot older, and having an older guy pay attention to me made me feel really good. I was feeling so guilty about it all, I wouldn't have blamed my sister for blaming me, too. So I just couldn't tell her, and I pulled away from her.

Before it happened to me I thought girls were just as strong as boys and that we could do anything they could do. I thought I was tougher than leather. But this put out my fire. It turned me against sports and made me feel like I was "just a girl." I felt really vulnerable and weak, but I was afraid NOT to be the strong one. I was afraid if I showed anyone how weak I was, I'd be taken advantage of again.

Being with guys was different for me, too. I still dated, I wasn't promiscuous, but I guess I felt like it was okay to have sex because I wasn't a virgin anymore and I didn't really have anything to save for someone special. So, if I was dating someone and we had sex, that was okay.

When I was 17, though, I got pregnant. I knew I wasn't ready to have a baby, and besides, I didn't want to marry that guy, so I decided to have an abortion. That was almost as awful for me as being raped in the first place. I felt just as violated and vulnerable, and the feelings of guilt and shame that followed were so much the same that I couldn't pretend I wasn't raped when I was 12.

A few weeks after the abortion, I arrived at my sister's house for Thanksgiving dinner. I was the first one there, and I just couldn't keep it inside me anymore. I had to tell her. I missed being close with my older sister, and I felt like I needed her more than ever right then. I started to cry, and it all came out. I told her about everything from her ex-boyfriend to the abortion. And I kept telling her how sorry I was for what happened.

She kept reassuring me that it wasn't my fault, and she said everything was going to be okay. She was absolutely supportive. She cried with me and said she was so sorry for our childhood rivalry. She said she was sad that I hadn't told her sooner. Then she said, "Please don't ever think there's anything you should hide from me."

Telling my sister made such a difference for me. She's the absolute greatest thing in the world and I don't know what I would have done without her.

If I could give advice to kids I'd say, "No matter what you are afraid of or feel guilty about, feeling alone can be resolved when you tell someone. You may be afraid the person you tell will think you're promiscuous or that you have caused what happened. But even if you doubt their response, even if the person you want to tell is the person you're most afraid to tell, tell someone you trust. Don't keep your secret bottled up inside you. Sexual abuse is not a secret, it should be screamed out loud sometimes and whispered to someone at other times. Regardless of the way you choose to tell, please tell! You are not alone unless you keep silent. Telling will allow you to get safe and begin to heal."

Hope's story shows how hard it can be to tell someone about sexual abuse. She struggled for a long time before finally telling her sister. You might also want to tell someone, but feel afraid to do so. Sometimes telling can be as hard as being abused. It can be embarrassing and scary, especially if you think you're responsible. You also might be worried about breaking up your family or afraid of making someone angry or jealous. You might also be worried about being blamed.

Unfortunately, there's no way to be sure someone won't get angry, blame you or say you could have stopped it. But remember, no matter what anyone says, it's never the child's fault. Sexual abusers do lots of things to trick or force kids into sexual activity, and they do even more things to keep kids quiet and keep the abuse ongoing.

That's why it's important for you to tell someone. Even if telling is the hardest thing for you, it's the only way to be sure you will get safe and stay safe. It's the only way to be sure other kids in your family, in your neighborhood, or in your school will get safe and stay safe, too.

Remember: Even though telling is hard, even though it's scary, you need to tell a trusting adult so you can get safe and stay safe.

Chapter 15

Hold on, You'll Be Okay

Darrell's Story

My name is Darrell. I'm 16 years old and in the tenth grade. Right now, I live in a group home. I lived in a foster home and had been the only child there until my older foster brother came. I was four or five and he was about seven or eight. We were cool at first. We got along like brothers should. Then things changed for the worse. Then, I don't know why, but he changed for the worse. He became angry and depressed, and he'd do things like burn his arm and accuse my foster parents of doing things to him. He wanted to leave the foster home. I think he thought he'd go home to his real family.

The abuse started about five or six months into his stay at the foster home. At first he'd just watch me; then he started touching me in a sexual way. Like when I got out of the bathtub, I'd go to my room, and that's when he would touch me. Eventually it grew from fondling into more and more stuff.

I didn't tell anyone at first because I didn't understand

what he was doing. As the younger brother, I thought I was doing something, to ask for it. But whenever I said I didn't want to do it, he'd tell me it was okay because we were just playing, like playing house, and this is what normal brothers did. If I was good, and I kept our secret, he'd buy me things and let me stay in his room and watch television or play video games.

Before he started doing it to me, I had a lot of friends. But after, I was afraid the other kids might find out what was going on. I was even more scared that they would try to do it to me, too. So, I stayed away from all the boys I used to play with, and if a boy wanted to be my friend or tried to get close to me, I'd say mean things to him as a defense to push him away from me.

I also stopped doing the things the other boys in the neighborhood or school were doing. I didn't play football or anything. I stayed in the house a lot, with my mom. That's how I got interested in music and dancing. My mom saw how much I liked music and asked me if I wanted to take dancing lessons. I did, and whenever she was busy, I'd listen to music and practice my jazz. It was a safe place where I could go and feel good about myself, and nobody bothered me.

Anyway, it went on until I was eight years old. That's when what my brother was saying just didn't fit with how I felt. I didn't think what we were doing was a game. It just didn't feel right, and I didn't want him to do it anymore. So I told my foster parents about it. They told me I was lying and that it couldn't have happened in their house. They said they would check it out, but they didn't. I know they asked my brother one time about it, and he denied it. They never did anything else about it. That really scared me because I kept thinking, "If they won't help me, then who will?"

So he kept abusing me, and I didn't know what to do. I'd just sit there and let it happen. I didn't want him to do it, but I didn't know what to do or where to go to hide from him. I didn't feel safe in the house. There wasn't anywhere I could go where I felt I could be away from him.

Finally, one day I told my caseworker. That was really scary for me, too, because I didn't know if she would believe me, either. She told me she'd talk to my foster parents. She said they denied it and that my foster brother denied it, too. I know he lied to her about it but she told me she couldn't do anything for me.

The more I thought about that, the angrier I got. I started doing things to make my foster parents look at me, notice me. I stabbed my brother with a fork and threw stuff around the house. I tore the house apart, jumped on my mom's bed and kicked stuff over. I wanted them to know that something was wrong. I wanted them to know I needed their help.

It took a little while, but finally my foster parents got me a counselor. I didn't come out and tell her what was going on, but she started asking me these questions, and that's when she found out. I told her, "My brother's doing things to me." I didn't know what it was called. She told my foster parents what was going on, and they still didn't do anything, so my counselor said she was going to do something about it.

She said she had to do something. She contacted my

caseworker. My caseworker came to the house, confronted my foster family and said there was an ongoing report of sexual abuse. I was removed from the home and went to another home, a co-worker of my foster mother. He was a single man whose son was grown. That wasn't too good, either.

As soon as I moved in, I knew something was wrong because of the way he talked to me. Right away, he started telling me how Michael Jackson had molested those boys and how he did it. I tried to stay out of the house, stay away from him, as much as I could, but when I came in at night, he'd be there, awake. I couldn't avoid him. He never forced me or anything, but the only television was in his room, so if I wanted to watch television or anything, I'd have to go into his room. And when I'd be in his room watching something he'd come in and promise me things like money and stuff. He'd tell me that if I went along with what he wanted, I'd have a nice life. I didn't know what else to do. I didn't have anywhere to go, and I knew no one would protect me.

I was with him about six months and still in counseling for what my brother did to me, when he admitted to the counselor that he was doing it, too. I don't know why he told her, but it made me feel good that he told the truth. Right away, the counselor told the caseworker, and she came and removed me from the house. I was put into a group home at that point, and that's where I am now, where I'll stay until I'm ready for college.

I've finished my counseling and that really helped me. My counselor taught me how to deal with my anger. And she helped me understand the mixed-up feelings I had about girls and my own sexuality. I didn't understand why I had mixed-up feelings, I knew I wasn't gay. But now I know that's normal for what I went through, and talking about it with someone I trusted really helped me sort things out for myself.

My counselor also helped me know what to do if I see these people again, because they still live close to me. She told me that if I see them, I should say "hi," but just keep walking and not get into a conversation or anything.

The kids at school make fun of me because I like dance instead of playing football, but I think what I have been through has made me stronger. I know that I am who I am and I'm okay with myself. I also think what I've been through has inspired me to become something. I want to become a lawyer and a counselor so I can defend kids as a child advocate.

If I had a chance to say something to adults, I'd say, "No matter how hard it might be, believe the kids who are coming to you, listen to them." And I would tell kids who were going through my predicament, "Hold on, hold on. You'll get through it eventually. Someone will be there for you, eventually, whether you think so or not."

❋ ❋ ❋

Most of the time, trusting adults believe the children who come to them. They act quickly to get kids safe. But as Darrell's story shows, sometimes that doesn't happen. He was sexually abused for a long time.

Like Darrell, it might take a long time for you to get safe, too. You might have to tell many people what happened before someone believes you or is able to help you. When you do find a trusting adult who can help, it might take time for them to learn what happened and decide what they need to do to protect you. But no matter how long it takes, hold on! You deserve to be safe and eventually you will be.

Remember: Getting safe doesn't always happen quickly. But, hang in there. Eventually someone will believe you and help you get safe.

Resources

Where to Go for Help

If someone has hurt you, or someone you care about, in a sexual way, you might feel confused and frightened. But stay calm. Don't panic and never confront the offender.

Report the incident immediately. Tell a trusting adult, talk with a teacher or call your local police, child protection services, child advocacy center, or sexual assault crisis center.

For the sexual assault crisis center closest to you contact:

Rape, Abuse & Incest National Network (RAINN)
635-B Pennsylvania Avenue S.E.
Washington, DC 20003
Phone: (800) 656-HOPE
Fax: (202) 544-3556
E-mail: info@rainn.org
Web: http://www.rainn.org

For more information contact:

Childhelp USA®
15757 N. 78th Street
Scottsdale, AZ 85260
National Child Abuse Hotline
Phone: (800) 4-A-CHILD
TDD/Hearing Impaired: (800) 2-A-CHILD
Fax: (480) 922-7061
Web: http://www.childhelpusa.org

Children Now
1212 Broadway, 5th Floor
Oakland, CA 94612
Phone: (510) 763-2444
Fax: (510) 763-1974
E-mail: children@childrennow.org
Web: http://www.childrennow.org

The Children's Defense Fund
25 E Street N.W.
Washington, DC 20001
Phone: (202) 628-8787
E-mail: cdfinfo@childrensdefense.org
Web: http://www.childrensdefense.org

Child Welfare League of America
Headquarters
440 First Street N.W., 3rd Floor
Washington, DC 20001-2085
Program Office
50 F Street N.W., 6th Floor
Washington, DC 20001-2085
Phone: (202) 638-2952
Fax: (202) 638-4004
Web: http://www.cwla.org

Federal Bureau of Investigation (FBI)
National Sex Offender Registries
J. Edgar Hoover Building
935 Pennsylvania Avenue N.W.
Washington, DC 20535-0001
Phone: (202) 324-3000
Web: http://www.fbi.gov/hq/cid/cac/registry.htm
FBI Field Office Information: http://www.fbi.gov/contact/
fo/info.htm

Kids Helping Kids Break the Silence of Sexual Abuse
P.O. Box 401
Bridgeville, PA 15017
Phone: (412) 628-5544
Fax: (412) 257-6042
E-mail: LindaFoltz@kidshelpkids.net
Web: http://www.kidshelpkids.net

Love Our Children USA™
220 East 57th Street
New York, NY 10022
Phone: (888) 301-5118
Fax: (212) 980-3110
E-mail: info@loveourchildrenusa.org
Web: http://www.loveourchildrenusa.org

The National Center for Victims of Crime
2000 M Street N.W., Suite 480
Washington, DC 20036
Phone: (800) FYI-CALL
TDD/Hearing Impaired: (800) 211-7996
Fax: (202) 467-8701
Web: http://www.ncvc.org
State Links: http://www.ncvc.org/links/Sl.htm

**National Clearinghouse
on Child Abuse and Neglect Information**
330 C Street S.W.
Washington, DC 20447
Phone: (800) FYI-3366
Fax: (708) 385-3206
Web: http://www.calib.com/nccanch

National Organization for Victim Assistance (NOVA)
1730 Park Road N.W.
Washington, DC 20010
Phone: (800) TRY-NOVA
Fax: (202) 462-2255
Web: http://www.try-nova.org

Office for Victims of Crime Resource Center
National Criminal Justice Reference Service
P.O. Box 6000
Rockville, MD 20849-6000
Phone: (800) 627-6872
TTY/Hearing Impaired: (877) 712-9279
E-mail: askovc@ojp.usdoj.gov
Web: http://www.ojp.usdoj.gov/ovc

Parents Anonymous® Inc.
675 W. Foothill Boulevard, Suite 220
Claremont, CA 91711
Phone: (909) 621-6184
Fax: (909) 625-6304
E-mail: parentsanonymous@parentsanonymous.org
Web: http://www.parentsanonymous.org

Prevent Child Abuse America (PCA America)
200 S. Michigan Avenue, 17th Floor
Chicago, IL 60604-2404
Phone: (312) 663-3520
Fax: (312) 939-8962
E-mail: mailbox@preventchildabuse.org
Web: http://www.preventchildabuse.org

Stand for Children
1420 Columbia Road N.W., 3rd Floor
Washington, DC 20009
Phone: (800) 663-4032
Fax: (202) 234-0391
E-mail: tellstand@stand.org
Web: http://www.stand.org

Resources

Freeman, Lory. *It's My Body: A Book to Teach Young Children How to Resist Uncomfortable Touch*. Seattle: Parenting Press, Inc., 1984.

Girard, Linda Walvoord. *My Body Is Private*. Nikes, Ill.: Albert Whitman & Co., 1992.

Hermes, Patricia. *A Solitary Secret*. New York: Harcourt Brace Jovanovich, 1985.

Kehoe, Patricia. *Something Happened and I'm Scared to Tell: A Book for Young Victims of Abuse*. Seattle: Parenting Press, Inc., 1987.

Russell, Pamela. *Do You Have A Secret? How to Get Help for Scary Secrets*. Minneapolis: CompCare Publishers, 1986.

Sanford, Doris. *I Can't Talk About It: A Child's Book About Sexual Abuse (A Corner of the Heart)*. Sisters, Ore.: Multnomah Publishers, Inc., 1986.

Spelman, Cornelia. *Your Body Belongs To You*. Morton Grove, Ill.: Albert Whitman & Co., 1997.

Resources

Adams, Caren and Jennifer Fay. *No More Secrets: Protecting Your Child from Sexual Assault*. San Luis Obispo, Calif.: Impact Publishers, Inc., 1981.

Colao, Flora and Tamar Hosansky. *Your Children Should Know: Personal Safety Strategies for Parents to Teach Their Children*. New York: Berkley Books, 1987.

Hagans, Kathyrn and Joyce Case. *When Your Child Has Been Molested: A Parent's Guide to Healing and Recovery*. San Francisco: Jossey-Bass, Inc., 1998.

Hart-Rossi, Janie. *Protect Your Child from Sexual Abuse: A Parent's Guide*. Seattle: Parenting Press, Inc., 1984.

Kraizer, Sherryll. *The Safe Child Book: A Commonsense Approach to Protecting Children and Teaching Children to Protect Themselves*. Simon & Schuster, Inc., 1996.

Murphy Ph.D., Tim and Loriann Hoff Oberlin. *The Angry Child: Regaining Control When Your Child is Out of Control*. New York: Clarkson Potter, 2001.

About the Author

Linda Lee Foltz is a survivor of childhood sexual abuse. After healing from the trauma of her own childhood, she wanted to "make a difference" and began volunteering at a child advocacy center. There she met hundreds of kids whose lives, like hers, were forever altered.

In her work, she learned that the only way to break the silence, stop the cycle and protect innocent children is through stronger educational tools. Victimized kids, through their heroic voices, their true stories and their amazing ability to survive, have the power to reach out and teach other kids in a dynamic new way. That became the idea for *Kids Helping Kids Break the Silence of Sexual Abuse.*

A child rights advocate, Foltz frequently speaks at national conferences and meetings, sharing her own personal struggle with sexual abuse, as well as some of the gripping stories from her book.

Although talks are tailored to meet the needs of the audience, suggested topics include: *Breaking the Silence*; *My Best Friend Just Told Me Something and I Don't Know What to Do*; and *What Parents Need to Know to Protect Their Children.*

For information on scheduling programs, please contact:

Linda Foltz
Kids Helping Kids
P. O. Box 401
Bridgeville, PA 15017
(412) 628-5544
www.kidshelpkids.net
LindaFoltz@kidshelpkids.net

Do You Have a Story of Triumph Over Adversity?

Would you like to help others learn from what you've endured, survived, and triumphed?

Linda Foltz is accepting true stories for future books about the following topics:

- Self-Destructive Behavior (eating disorders, cutting, etc.)
- Physical Abuse and Abandonment
- Drugs and Alcohol
- Violence, Guns and Gangs
- Teen Pregnancy
- Depression and Suicide

For consideration, please email:
LindaFoltz@kidshelpkids.net

Interviewees are compensated and must sign a release. Anyone under 18 years of age must have signed parental permission.

Order Form

Kids Helping Kids
Break the Silence of Sexual Abuse
By Linda Lee Foltz

Retail Price: Softcover $14.95 U.S.
                              Hardcover $21.95 U.S.

Special Offer: 2 Softcover for $26.90 U.S. (*Save 10%*)
                              2 Hardcover for $39.50 U.S. (*Save 10%*)

Shipping:

Book Rate: Add $3.50 for shipping for first book
                              and $1.25 for each additional book.
                              (Surface shipping may take three to
                              four weeks.)

Priority Shipping: $9.00 for up to two books (Please call
                              for priority shipping on more than two
                              books. Phone: 412-323-9320)

Terms: Payment with order.

Please send me _____ (Please circle: Softcover or Hardcover) books. I
understand that I may return any book for a full refund – for any reason,
no questions asked.

Name:_____

Address:_____

City:_____ State:_____ Zip:_____

Sales Tax: Please add 7% for books shipped to Pennsylvania addresses.

Amount enclosed: _____

Send check or money order to:
Lighthouse Point Press
100 First Avenue, Suite 525
Pittsburgh, PA 15222